A·Q·U·A·M·A·S·T·E·R ™

— *Tim Hayes • Tristan Lougher • Dick Mills* —

MARINE
AQUARIUMS

D0873801

BOWTIE
P R E S S®

A Division of BowTie, Inc.
Irvine, California

First published in the USA and Canada by BowTie Press®
A Division of BowTie, Inc.
3 Burroughs
Irvine, CA 92618
www.bowtiepress.com

Originally published in 2006
© 2006 Interpet Publishing
Vincent Lane, Dorking, Surrey
RH4 3YX, England

Library of Congress Cataloging-in-Publication Data

Hayes, Tim.
  Marine aquariums / by Tim Hayes, Tristan Lougher, and
Dick Mills.
     p. cm. — (Aquamaster)
  ISBN 1-931993-82-3
  1. Marine aquariums. I. Lougher, Tristan. II. Mills, Dick. III.
Title. IV. Title.

SF457.1.H38 2006
639.34'2—dc22

2006020096

Created and compiled: Ideas into Print, Claydon,
Suffolk, IP6 0AB, England
Design and prepress: Stuart Watkinson, Ayelands,
New Ash Green, DA3 8JW, England
Computer graphics: Phil Holmes and Stuart Watkinson
Principal photography: Geoffrey Rogers
© Interpet Publishing
Production management: Consortium, Poslingford,
Suffolk CO10 8RA, England
Print production: Sino Publishing House Ltd., Hong Kong

Printed and bound in China
10 9 8 7 6 5 4 3 2 1

Additional material supplied by Andrew Caine,
Dave Garratt, Steve Halls, and Lisa Page.

Contents

Meeting the challenge

If your fish-keeping experience has been confined to tropical freshwater fish, you should consider a number of factors before embarking on the challenge of setting up a marine aquarium. Firstly, bear in mind that the coral reef environment is very stable, and marine fish have not evolved mechanisms to deal with unstable conditions in captivity. Secondly, pathogenic organisms do not abound on the reef, so once again, marine fish are ill equipped to deal with outbreaks of disease in the close confines of the aquarium. You will find that the number of fish you can keep in a tank of any given size is far fewer than you have been used to and that aquarium plants will not feature in the system. Finally, you will need to think about the kind of aquarium you plan to set up: fish-only; live-rock–based fish-only, or a reef aquarium. However, if you are prepared to meet the exacting demands placed on the marine fish-keeper, the rewards are well worth it.

A FISH-ONLY MARINE SETUP

A fish-only tank will usually contain either larger fish species or those that would prey on invertebrates, such as corals, crustaceans, and mollusks. Often, aquarists use inert rock for aquascaping because of the perceived likelihood that at some point they will have to use copper-based medications, which are toxic to invertebrates.

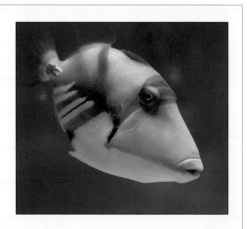

* Live rock can be used in a fish-only setup instead of inert rock. Although this precludes the use of copper-based medications, because the live rock is home to large populations of small invertebrate animals, it plays an important part in filtration and provides a healthier environment for fish, which can browse on it.

LEARN ALL YOU CAN

Investigate all the key issues associated with the hobby, such as maturation of a biological filter, fish and invertebrate compatibility, correct diet and feeding, stocking levels, and the natural behavior of the species you hope to keep. This vital information will prove invaluable in your marine hobby.

A REEF AQUARIUM

In a reef aquarium, the emphasis is on keeping a display of corals with a few small, compatible fish plus sundry non-predatory, mobile invertebrates. Most of the animals found in the marine hobby are collected from different types of coral reef, so it makes sense to research where your fish have come from and then house a selection of animals with the same requirements in terms of water movement, levels of lighting, and substrate.

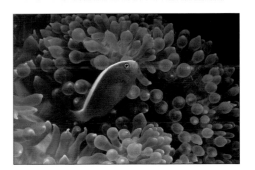

* Decide which animals you want to keep. If the answer is clownfish (anemonefish) and anemones, the reef design will be quite different from one that would suit small-polyped stony corals, such as Acropora species. This, in turn, will dictate your aquascaping, lighting, and water flow requirements and your companion fish and invertebrate species.

▲ *An orange skunk clownfish* (Amphiprion sandaracinos) *nestles inside a bubble anemone* (Entacmaea quadricolor). *The interaction between clownfish and their hosts is always attractive to watch.*

◀ *Most fish and invertebrates are collected from all over the world. A geographically themed reef would be dedicated to fish and invertebrates collected from, say, the Caribbean, the Red Sea, or Hawaii.*

Living in a salt solution

The key differences between marine fish and freshwater fish, both cold-water and tropical, are the level of salt found in the water they inhabit and their ability to survive in that environment. The process by which the salts are absorbed and excreted from the fish's bodies and the way in which they control salt levels is known as osmoregulation.

MARINE FISH

Marine fish differ from freshwater fish in the way they balance the levels of salts and fluids in their bodies. The marine environment has a higher salt level than is found in the body fluids of marine fish. As a result, they face a constant battle against dehydration, as water is lost to the surrounding seawater and salts are retained in the body. Marine fish deal with this situation by consuming large amounts of water and excreting very little urine. Only a few salts are absorbed from the seawater they drink; chloride cells in the gills actively excrete salt.

▲ *Marine fish are well adapted to thrive in a highly salty environment. They can absorb water and excrete the salt to maintain their internal body fluids at the right concentration.*

FRESHWATER FISH

The bodies of freshwater fish contain higher levels of salts than in the surrounding water. There is a tendency for salts to be lost through the tissues as water flows in. To combat this, freshwater fish have extremely efficient kidneys that are able to excrete water very quickly while reabsorbing salts from the urine. In addition, their specially structured gills allow them to retain salts circulating in the blood that have been ingested with food.

▲ *A freshwater fish must excrete water constantly so that it does not burst.*

FRESHWATER FISH

Water passes by osmosis from the relatively dilute fresh water into the fish's body.

Salts pass out by diffusion.

The body fluids have a higher salt concentration than the surrounding water.

Kidneys excrete water and retain salts.

Chloride cells in the gills retain salts from water flowing over them.

Fish excrete large amounts of very dilute urine.

SALTWATER FISH

Water passes by osmosis from the relatively dilute fish's body out into the sea.

Salts pass in by diffusion.

The body fluids have a lower salt concentration than the surrounding water.

Huge quantities of water are swallowed.

Water, but not salts, are absorbed in the gut.

Salts are actively eliminated by the gills.

A small amount of urine is produced.

CHOOSING AND PLACING A TANK

Choosing and placing a tank

There are various very attractively shaped tank designs on the market, including bow-fronted aquariums. Always choose the largest aquarium you can afford and accommodate. Opt for a tank no less than 3 ft (90 cm) long, with a capacity of 36 gallons (136 liters). The larger the tank, the less effect any fluctuations in water conditions will have on marine life. Bear in mind that a tank filled with water and aquarium decor will be extremely heavy and must be placed on a firm base supported on a strong floor. Try to arrange an even distribution of weight across floor joists. Cushion the tank against any unevenness in the stand with a sheet of polystyrene or plastic foam.

▲ *Compare the difference in size between a starter freshwater tank (left) and a first marine aquarium.*

▼ With a marine tank, especially a reef tank, maximize the breadth (front to back measurement) to reduce the optical foreshortening effect that you get in a water-filled aquarium. The deeper the tank (top to bottom), the more lighting you need. Bear in mind that deep tanks are difficult to service.

* While you are choosing your main display tank, buy another, smaller tank to use as a separate quarantine tank.

▶ *Use this formula to calculate the capacity of your aquarium: Length (L) x breadth (B) x depth (D) in feet (centimeters), divided by 1,000, gives you the volume in gallons (liters). Live rock and other decor will displace the water, so reduce the volume by approximately 10 percent.*

TANK SIZES AND CAPACITIES

Tank size (LxBxD)	Volume of water
3x1.5x1.25 ft (90x40x38 cm)	36 gal (136 L)
3x1.5x1.5 ft (90x45x45 cm)	48 gal (182 L)
3.3x1.5x1.5 ft (100x45x4 5cm)	54 gal (203 L)
4x1.5x1.5 ft (120x45x45 cm)	64 gal (243 L)
4x2x1.5 ft (120x60x45 cm)	86 gal (324 L)
5x2x2 ft (150x60x60 cm)	143 gal (540 L)
6x2x2 ft (183x60x60 cm)	174 gal (660 L)

CHOOSING A GOOD LOCATION

Place the tank where it will enjoy stable conditions in a spot away from drafts and vibrations from TV or stereo equipment. There must be easy access to an electrical outlet. Do not place the tank in direct sunlight or close to a window in a room that receives the midday sun. Adequate ventilation in the room will help keep temperatures down in summer. Avoid a place close to where toxic fumes, such as from a central heating boiler duct, could be drawn back into the tank via an air pump. Place the tank away from common walkways through the house.

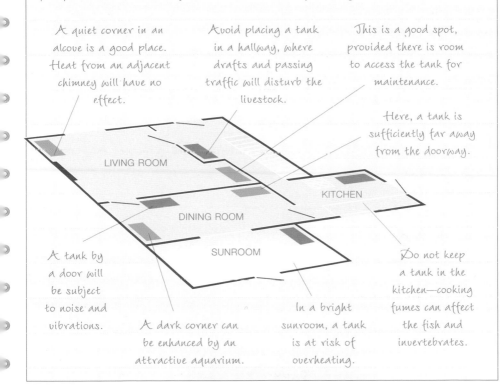

A quiet corner in an alcove is a good place. Heat from an adjacent chimney will have no effect.

Avoid placing a tank in a hallway, where drafts and passing traffic will disturb the livestock.

This is a good spot, provided there is room to access the tank for maintenance.

Here, a tank is sufficiently far away from the doorway.

LIVING ROOM

KITCHEN

DINING ROOM

SUNROOM

A tank by a door will be subject to noise and vibrations.

A dark corner can be enhanced by an attractive aquarium.

In a bright sunroom, a tank is at risk of overheating.

Do not keep a tank in the kitchen—cooking fumes can affect the fish and invertebrates.

* Leave enough space around the tank for essential maintenance. Keep all the cords neat and tidy, and label each one clearly.

◀ Decide at the outset whether to house all the tank hardware in a fail-safe sump tank beneath the main tank, thus maximizing swimming space.

AQUARIUM FURNISHING

Aquarium furnishing

In modern marine aquariums, the substrate and rocks play an integral role in maintaining water quality and provide the fish and invertebrates with a habitat to live in or on. Coral sand and gravel are the most suitable and easily available substrates. Select rocks of calcareous origin, such as limestone or coral, to avoid the risk of introducing unsuitable materials that may react with salt water and prove toxic to livestock. Live rock is highly porous and capable of supporting large populations of bacteria, along with small organisms such as algae, crustaceans, and mollusks. These animals help to turn the captive reef into a diverse, natural system, while the bacteria process organic wastes produced by the fish and other, larger animals.

◀ *Ocean rock is suitable for a fish-only setup. Being a dense material, it displaces quite a lot of water.*

◀ *Coral sand and gravel help maintain a stable pH and high buffering capacity.*

LIVE ROCK

Look for rock of low density, preferably pieces showing signs of interesting life, such as tube worms, calcareous algae, and macroalgae. Do not expect to find corals. If you are building a reef on a budget, start with a limited amount of good-quality live rock, and then build up the reef with well-cured pieces as you can afford them. The live rock is the infrastructure on which to build up the reef; leave room for adding corals later on. Position the largest pieces at the bottom of the aquarium and work upward, using incrementally smaller pieces. Leave spaces between them for both the animals and free water movement. Step back to check on your design.

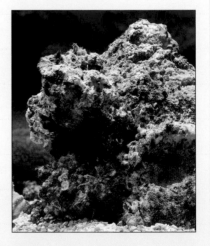

▲ *Live rock, a natural, renewable resource, is mainly composed of coral rubble resulting from storm damage.*

◀ *There are products (often egg-crate types made of PVC) available that provide tiers on which to arrange corals or rocks. The acrylic racks shown here are common in the United Kingdom.*

ARTIFICIAL DECOR FOR A FISH-ONLY SYSTEM

If you are maintaining clownfish in a fish-only aquarium, an artificial anemone can help them feel more secure in the company of larger fish. Imitation corals and sponges provide extra color. Coral reproductions with an elongate, tree, or branchlike structure contrast well with rocks.

This is an imitation anemone made of silicone rubber.

An artificial sea fan can look surprisingly realistic.

A synthetic stony coral will soon blend in.

* When designing a habitat, take into account the needs of the animals you wish to keep. By including caves, crevices, arches, and overhanging ledges, plus plenty of swimming space, you can cater to a wide range of creatures.

AQUARIUM FURNISHING

Temperature control

The water in a marine aquarium must be maintained at a reasonably constant temperature if fish and invertebrates from tropical coral reefs are to survive. In a fish-only aquarium, the general guide is to allow 2 watts per quart (liter) of water, with the total wattage required being split between two Heaterstats in large tanks. Even if little used, you should have a heater. In a reef aquarium of modest size (say, 53 gallons [200 liters]), heating is required to bring the water up to temperature when you first start off the reef; but subsequently, in the average house, heaters will be doing very little work except on the coldest nights. Because of the amount of lighting used above a reef tank to illuminate the corals, it is more likely that you will encounter problems in keeping the temperature below the maximum tolerated by tropical marine organisms.

A Heaterstat is a small individual immersion heater combined with a thermostat control.

Use the holder to keep the heating element away from the glass.

A plastic shield protects the base of the glass tube.

▲ A large reef aquarium may not need a heater. While it is lit during the day, heat from the lights is transferred to the water, where it is stored.

* As many fish enjoy resting on underwater obstacles, fit a guard over the heater to prevent them from burning themselves. This is essential with slow-moving animals, such as anemones, echinoderms, and mollusks.

◀ To check water temperatures around the tank, fix a number of external stick-on LCD thermometers at varying depths. Adjust the position of powerheads (water pumps) to eliminate any cold areas.

COOLING THE WATER

Overheating is becoming more common, especially with the trend toward increased levels of lighting. Installing a cooler is the sophisticated way of dealing with the problem. There are three main cooler designs: those based on the use of refrigerant gas, those based on evaporative cooling, and those based on the peltier element (thermoelectric). The last option is the cheapest but the least efficient and suitable only for smaller tanks.

▶ *Refrigerant coolers are the most expensive option but are highly efficient and easy to plumb. Some units have additional features: for example, they may also act as a heater or incorporate a built-in UV sterilizer.*

◀ *Evaporative coolers are efficient and economical, but you must run an auto top-off system in conjunction with them to deal with the additional evaporation. Vent them outdoors to reduce room humidity.*

▶ *In an emergency, float plastic bags or a food-safe container of ice in the aquarium. Alternatively, freeze the RO (reverse osmosis) water used for topping off evaporation losses, and allow it to melt in the tank.*

TEMPERATURE CONTROL

Lighting the aquarium

Lighting a fish-only aquarium is a matter of personal taste. Two fluorescent tubes will usually suffice, with perhaps a third, blue lamp for night viewing. However, if there are invertebrates in the tank, lighting becomes far more important. Many corals, anemones, and mollusks rely on microscopic algae, known as zooxanthellae, for food. After good water quality, the main requirement of zooxanthellae is high-intensity light at the correct wavelength. In a reef aquarium, the correct lighting is therefore of paramount importance, and this usually means using high-output T5 tubes or metal-halide lamps.

▼ Actinic tubes give out light that peaks in the blue part of the spectrum. This light is particularly appreciated by invertebrates, including corals. Actinic tubes are often fitted in conjunction with white tubes and switched on before (and switched off after) the white tubes to simulate dawn and dusk lighting. This can also be less stressful for the fish.

▲ Traditional T8 fluorescent tubes (top) are 1 inch (25 mm) wide and available in various colors. T5 tubes (center) are 0.5 in (16 mm) in diameter and provide a brighter light output for their size. These are also available in a compact PL format (bottom), in which the tube is bent back on itself and has four connecting pins at one end of the fitting.

Clip–on reflectors help to maximize the effect of fluorescent light by directing most of it down into the water.

METAL-HALIDE LIGHTING

If unit size or heat output is of little concern, then the light produced by metal halide systems is closest to that experienced by corals in their natural environment. The lamps are defined by the energy they require (e.g., 150-, 250-, and 400-watt) and by the color temperature of light they emit, measured in degrees Kelvin (°K). A 13,000K 150-watt lamp is good for an aquarium up to 23.5 in (60 cm) deep with a mix of hard and soft corals. If you wish to keep mostly stony corals in the same aquarium, opt for a 250-watt or even a 400-watt unit to compensate for the light absorbed by the water.

▲ *Metal-halide lighting units are essential if you plan to keep hard corals, clams, and other invertebrates that require high light levels. However, they are costly; if this is a problem, consider keeping a fish-only tank until funds are available for metal halides.*

MAXIMIZING YOUR LIGHTING

Light is emitted in all directions. Reflectors direct it into the tank.

If used, keep condensation trays clean to reduce light absorption.

Particles in the water absorb a large amount of light.

Some light is lost through the glass.

Corals and other invertebrates need to receive high levels of illumination.

◀ *Even well-directed light can be wasted if the cover glass is dirty. Keep everything spotlessly clean.*

* Some corals can be adversely affected by sudden exposure to more powerful lighting. Suspend a metal-halide unit farther above the tank than normal, and lower it gradually over several days.

Water management

The best way of providing suitable water for the marine aquarium is to use an artificial salt mix that is carefully balanced and combined with good-quality tap water so that the final composition approximates natural seawater as closely as possible. For the reef aquarium, it is particularly important to make salt water using fresh water containing as few nutrients as possible. By limiting undesirable nutrients such as phosphates and nitrates from the very start, you have a far better chance of keeping a reef aquarium without constantly battling against pest algae. RO (reverse osmosis) water is a good option. You can treat water by passing it through your own RO unit or buy it from your aquarium dealer, who will fill up a container for you. At the very least, pass domestic tap water through an aquarium nitrate-removing resin.

* For the reef tank, aim for natural seawater levels of salt, recognized as a salinity of 35 ppt (1 oz [35 gm] of salt per quart [liter] of water).

▶ A reverse osmosis unit removes contaminants from tap water.

THE pH VALUE

The pH of water is a measure of its acidity or alkalinity. It is measured on a logarithmic scale; 7 is the neutral value. Values below 7 are acidic, while above 7 they are alkaline. Seawater has a higher pH than most fresh water and domestic tap water and should be maintained at 8.3. A falling pH indicates that the water quality is deteriorating, usually due to an increase in carbon dioxide production because of a buildup of organic debris and because the water's buffering capacities (its ability to resist pH changes) is declining. A 25% water change restores the pH to its normal value. An increase in carbon dioxide (CO_2) levels can also result from insufficient water surface movement or a lack of ventilation.

▶ Because the pH scale is logarithmic, each unit change is a change times ten. Sudden changes are stressful to fish.

pH 9

pH 8

pH 7

SPECIFIC GRAVITY AND SALINITY

The terms *specific gravity* (SG) and *salinity* can cause confusion. SG (a measure of density) is often used within the marine hobby as a means of assessing the saltiness of the water. However, the correlation between specific gravity and salinity depends on temperature, which means you would get different readings of SG from the same sample of water tested over a range of different temperatures. Salinity is a measure of how much salt is in the water—usually expressed as parts per thousand (ppt)—the same as ounces per gallon (grams per liter).

▼ *A refractometer is another means of measuring salinity. It automatically compensates for temperature and gives a reading in parts per thousand. (An electronic handheld meter is very accurate but expensive.)*

▼ *Hydrometers measure the amount of salt in the water in terms of SG. They give an accurate measurement only within a narrow temperature range, which must be appropriate to that of your tank. This is a swing-arm model.*

Place a water sample on the viewing window.

The edge of the blue area shows the salinity.

WATER MANAGEMENT

WATER MANAGEMENT

Water management (continued)

When setting up an aquarium, you can choose between a total or a customized system. A total system incorporates integral filters, heating, and lighting. It may also include a variety of water management aids, such as a protein skimmer, calcium reactor, UV sterilizer, and denitrifying unit. The customized system set up on pages 22–27 uses separate pieces of equipment to achieve the three main types of filtration: biological, mechanical, and chemical. It features an externally fitted fluidized bed sand filter for biological filtration, an external protein skimmer for removing organic and chemical waste, and an external power sponge filter to help remove particles in suspension and to improve water movement.

A FLUIDIZED BED SAND FILTER

* Be aware that fluidized beds and biological filtration in canister filters may not be suitable for the reef aquarium.

◀ *A fluidized bed sand filter in a fish-only system has an amazing nitrifying capacity, but the efficiency of the bacteria involved depletes the oxygen content of the water flowing through the unit. Always aerate the water as it returns to the aquarium, either by introducing air into the return tube or by using a spray bar to distribute the water over the surface.*

A PROTEIN SKIMMER

▶ *A protein skimmer removes harmful organic substances from the aquarium before they can cause water quality to deteriorate. In the reaction chamber, a flow of tank water is in close contact with rising columns of air bubbles. Protein waste molecules stick to the bubble surfaces and are carried upward toward a skimmer cup, where the bubbles collapse, leaving a yellowish liquid that can be removed. Water should be drawn into the skimmer from as near the surface as possible.*

AN EXTERNAL POWER FILTER

Shut-off taps disconnect the filter without water spillage.

Plastic tubes carry water to and from the aquarium.

Incoming water passes upward through the filter media, packed in a plastic basket inside the canister. Maintain water flow at all times to prevent the media from turning anaerobic, as would quickly happen after any failure of the power supply.

An electric water pump is housed in the top part of the filter.

A TRICKLE FILTER

If room exists, you can build a simple drip-through trickle filter or tower above the sump in a fish-only system. It is a very efficient form of biological filtration, providing maximum oxygenation and superior nitrification compared with submerged biological filters. Trickle filters cause increased evaporation and consequent heat loss, which can be an advantage or disadvantage depending on the requirements of your system.

The spray bar delivers prefiltered water.

Filter wool

Water trickles through media trays, where it is exposed to air.

Efficient bacterial conversion of wastes occurs on the high surface area of biomedia.

Water management (continued)

Traditional methods of man-made biological filtration are neither advisable nor necessary in a reef aquarium. At the simplest level, all that is needed for a reef aquarium to work is lighting and water flow appropriate to the species being kept. Live rock, mud, or deep sand beds (DSB) are the best way of completing the nitrogen cycle in the reef aquarium.

WATER MANAGEMENT

THE BERLIN METHOD

The Berlin method combines protein skimming and the corresponding nitrifying and denitrifying actions of bacteria on the surface and internal interstices of live rock. It is much nearer to a "natural" method of water management in a reef aquarium than are other methods using man-made biological filtration.

* When using live rock as the basis of a reef aquarium, there is no need to add anything for the maturation process. The bioload of the live rock will take care of that itself.

A DEEP SAND BED (DSB) FILTER

The first compartment absorbs energy of the water flow from the display tank.

Water returns to the display tank.

Bed of fine coral sand 4—6 in (10—15 cm) deep

◄ The philosophy behind the deep sand bed (DSB) as used in reef aquariums is very close to that of the Berlin system, but the emphasis here is on a sand bed, 4 in (10 cm) or more deep, to do the natural filtration and denitrification work of live rock. In theory, the vast surface area offered by a DSB will far exceed that offered by a conventional live rock system, allowing you to considerably reduce the volume of tank taken up by rock. To work successfully, a DSB must be populated by plenty of small "creatures," or infauna; various worms and microcrustaceans; plus meiofauna predominantly the microbial colonies living on the sand. This is easy to achieve by seeding the bed with half a quart (liter) or so of sand from an established reef system.

THE MUD SYSTEM

The mud system is a natural form of filtration for a reef aquarium that utilizes a fine substrate, lit twenty-four hours a day, where macro-algae in the form of *Caulerpa* are grown. It does not require a protein skimmer or activated carbon to purify the water. It keeps the water well oxygenated through the photosynthesis of the *Caulerpa*, which, being constantly lit, helps to stabilize pH. This method uses the end products of fish metabolism and fixes them into plant tissue, thus preventing the accumulation of ammonia, nitrites, nitrates, and phosphates. The *Caulerpa* prevents the growth of undesirable hair algae by competing for essential nutrients; it can be physically harvested to remove nutrients from the system and can be used as a fresh food for fish. (See caution on p. 37.)

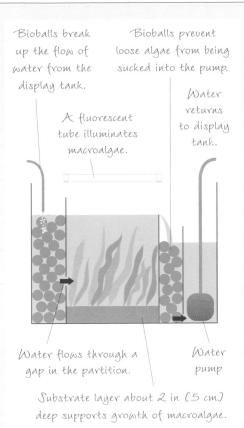

Bioballs break up the flow of water from the display tank.

Bioballs prevent loose algae from being sucked into the pump.

A fluorescent tube illuminates macroalgae.

Water returns to display tank.

Water flows through a gap in the partition.

Water pump

Substrate layer about 2 in (5 cm) deep supports growth of macroalgae.

USING CARBON

Carbon will remove the toxic compounds produced by soft corals for the purpose of chemical warfare against rival species, as well as clear up any discoloration of the water. There are three common strategies for using it: for twenty-four hours once a month; for seven days once a month; or continuously, replacing it regularly, preferably every six weeks or less. If carbon is used for extended periods, it will start to perform as a biological filter, with the risk of elevated nitrates. Even if you do not use it regularly, it is worth keeping some carbon on hand in the event of any emergency in which the aquarium water has become polluted. Place the carbon after the mechanical filtration stage so that it does not become clogged.

Setting up an aquarium

First, make a list of all the essential items and all the jobs you will need to carry out. It is useful to prepare your salt water mixture in advance of setting up. If you intend to introduce live rock at the setup stage, you cannot make the initial mix directly in the tank. If live rock is to be added a few days later, then it is probably more convenient to mix the salt water in the aquarium. Make sure that any substrate and rock work you plan to use in the display are sufficiently cleaned. (This does not apply to live rock.)

INSTALLING THE TECHNICAL EQUIPMENT

1 Place two heaters at opposite ends of the tank for even distribution and to safeguard against heater failure. Elements must not be covered by substrate.

SAFETY FIRST

- Choose a site for the tank that is near an electrical power outlet and is easily accessible, both for setting up and maintenance.
- Leave plenty of space for pieces of equipment around the tank.
- Fit a GFCI circuit breaker.
- Do not plug any equipment into the electrical supply until the tank is filled with water.
- Avoid tangling up electrical cords, and place connections away from water and splashes.
- Label plugs for future reference.

2 Place the return pipe from the external power filter at one end of the tank, where it can be hidden by decor.

3 Place the inlet filter pipe at the opposite end of the tank from the return pipe for efficient water circulation.

4 Connect hoses to the external power filter. Fit these securely so that they do not come apart when the filter is running under full pressure; otherwise, water in the tank will end up on the floor!

SETTING UP AN AQUARIUM

5 Securely connect the hoses to the external filter without tangling them. It helps to mark them IN and OUT.

6 If you place the aquarium on a cabinet, it is easy to hide external equipment, such as this external power filter.

7 This protein skimmer hangs on the back panel of the tank. Place it so that the correct operating water level is no lower than that of the aquarium; otherwise, it will overflow. Leave easy access for cleaning.

8 This tank incorporates a fluidized bed sand filter. This unit is driven by a small submersible water pump. Attach it inside the tank on the back glass. If possible, place the sand filter and protein skimmer at opposite ends.

9 Hang the fluidized sand bed filter on the outside of the back glass, and connect it to the internal pump with a hose. Be sure to fit the chamber containing the sand vertically.

Protein skimmer

Fluidized sand bed filter

Heating unit

Heating unit

Water return from external power filter

Intake for external power filter

Setting up an aquarium (continued)

In this setup, the decor will serve two purposes: one is to provide cover and territory for the inhabitants, and the other is to hide the equipment you have installed. If you cannot afford to create the habitat entirely from live rock, then construct the base features using a cheaper, inert rock. Leave space for any pieces of live rock you propose to add later on. Providing you have a supply of previously matured salt water on hand that has the correct temperature, specific gravity, and pH of 8.3, you can now introduce your pieces of live rock. Add the matured water immediately after placing your rocks and laying the substrate. Work carefully but quickly so that the live rock does not dry out. If you only have newly mixed salt water available at the setting-up stage, wait until the aquarium is fully operational before adding the live rock to avoid damaging the organisms in it.

ADDING THE DECOR

10 Fit a background to the outside of the back glass to hide the equipment. Fish and invertebrate colors stand out well against blue or black.

11 Add the first pieces of live rock directly onto the tank floor. Place them carefully so that you can build up a stable display. In this setup, we are using high-quality living rock, with no other form of base rock or other decor.

12 Create a habitat that provides retreats as well as open swimming space for those fish that require it. Do not allow the live rock to dry out.

13 Spread coral sand around the base of the tank and against the rocks to create a natural effect.

ADDING THE WATER

If you have already matured the water, then it is simply a case of carefully pouring it into the tank. It is a good idea to pour it onto a rock or into a container placed on the substrate to avoid moving the sand out of place.

If you do not have pre-matured water ready, mix a new batch before setting up. Use a spare heaterstat in the mixing container to bring the water temperature up to 75°F (24°C) so the salts will dissolve more readily. Once the salts are completely dissolved, take a specific gravity reading. If it is low, add more salts while taking further specific gravity tests until the SG is 1.022–1.023.

▼ *Look out for nitrate- and phosphate-free salt mixes and follow the manufacturer's directions exactly. Always use a nonmetallic container in which to mix the marine salts with water. Keep a suitable bucket solely for aquarium use. Food-quality plastic buckets are best.*

14 Pour the water gently onto the rocks to avoid displacing the sand. Connect the heating and filtration equipment to the electrical supply, and turn it on. Top off the water level if necessary. Monitor the water quality, and do not introduce any livestock until ammonia and nitrate levels have been zero for several days.

15 Attach the readout unit of a digital thermometer to the outer glass, and place the probe in the water, ideally some distance away from heating units.

Setting up an aquarium (continued)

In this setup, the lighting canopy is to be fitted with two white 10,000°K fluorescent tubes and one blue actinic 03. You should also be able to cut sections out of the hood to allow filter fittings, hoses, and cords to be routed through. A wooden hood laminated with plastic or painted with several coats of polyurethane varnish is ideal. Place any control gear for the lamps away from water and splashes. It is worth connecting the power cords for the lights into a remote-control box or power strip with the pumps and heaters so that there is only one cord running to the electrical outlet.

ADDING LIGHTS AND MATURING THE TANK

16 Make sure that fluorescent tubes are secured properly into the hood by clips designed for this purpose. Do not use metal clips.

17 Position the tubes in the hood (blue at the back) so they provide the best coverage within the aquarium. Place each tube as far away as possible from its neighbor to allow for good air circulation, which prevents overheating.

Two triphosphor white tubes

One actinic 03 blue tube

ALTERNATIVE OPTIONS

The fluidized sand bed filter, protein skimmer, and heater units could be fitted into a sump in a cabinet. Fit an overflow from the aquarium to the sump to return water to the aquarium. To improve water movement, install extra pumps, such as small powerheads, in the tank, hiding them behind the habitat. Consider including a UV (ultraviolet light) sterilizer to help maintain excellent water clarity and reduced numbers of pathogens.

MATURING THE FILTERS

Even though there are no animals in the aquarium at this stage, leave the lights on for the normal photoperiod (twelve hours per day) to help the maturation process. It is essential once uncured live rock has been introduced.

Do not introduce any more livestock into the aquarium until the filters have matured. This means waiting until there is a large enough population of nitrifying bacteria to deal with ammonia and nitrite. The presence of bacteria in uncured live rock may speed up the process; otherwise, you'll need to introduce the bacteria. Make daily tests for ammonia and nitrite levels until readings show zero for both. Wait until you have had several consecutive days of zero readings before adding livestock. Change 20–25% of the salt water to dilute the resulting levels of nitrate levels that may form.

▶ *It is vital to understand how the levels of nitrogenous waste products rise and fall during the first few weeks.*

Ammonia
As the initial decomposition processes begin, ammonia is formed and builds up quite quickly to a peak before gradually declining.

Nitrite
The second phase, the oxidation of ammonia to nitrite, soon follows, also peaking and then steadily falling away.

Nitrate
Oxidation of nitrite produces less harmful nitrate.

WEEK 1   WEEK 2   WEEK 3   WEEK 4   WEEK 5

THE MATURING AQUARIUM

▶ *Monitor water quality before adding any fish. Introducing a "cleaning gang" of hermit crabs or snails controls any developing algae growth while the tank is fish free and lit for 12 hours a day.*

Choosing fish

Several factors must influence your choice of fish for the aquarium: their compatibility, both with their own kind and unrelated species; their diet; their tolerance of captivity; their appearance; and even their cost. Be sure to research thoroughly all the species you would like to keep. Make sure your information is up to date; improvements in factors such as filtration, diet, specimen capture, and transport have all made it easier to keep species once considered "difficult."

MAKE A LIST

Well in advance of first stocking, make a list of fish species you would like to obtain, now and in the future. Show this to a knowledgeable dealer who can help you minimize territoriality and aggression issues before they arise. Devise a stocking order, starting with the hardier choices and finishing with the most delicate or territorial species.

▲ *Examine the fish you intend to buy, and observe their breathing rate. Avoid fish that appear to be panting. Do not necessarily ignore a fish with slightly split or damaged fins that is otherwise healthy and feeding. Fins can repair in a few days.*

FINS ON A MARINE FISH

Dorsal fin
This is the main "keel" to prevent the fish from rolling while swimming.

Pectoral fin (paired)
Many fish use these fins to help steer and change position.

Caudal fin (tail)
Most fish swim by sweeping the back part of the body from side to side. The tail fin helps to convert that movement into forward thrust.

Anal fin
This single fin acts as a stabilizer.

Pelvic fin (paired)
These also help the fish to control its position. Some triggerfish, filefish, and boxfish lack pelvic fins.

CHOOSING FISH

STOCKING LEVELS

As a guide to stocking a reef system, allow 1 in (2.5 cm) of fish per 6 gallons (23 liters). In a fish-only system, allow 1 in (2.5 cm) of fish per 3 gallons (11.5 liters). Stick to these levels for the first year. Your chances of success are greatly enhanced if you take a conservative approach while the tank is maturing and stabilizing.

▼ Dealers' fish are always juveniles, and most will grow much larger. This panther grouper (Chromileptes altivelis) is very appealing as a 2 in (5 cm) juvenile, but less so once it has rapidly grown into a 9 in (23 cm) predator.

REEF-FRIENDLY FISH

When starting out with a first reef aquarium, choose species of a size proportionate to the size of the tank. For the first year or so, stick to easy-to-keep, small, compatible, reef-friendly fish, such as small planktivores and small herbivores. It is also worth introducing species that undertake a useful role, such as the yellow sailfin tang (Zebrasoma flavescens) that grazes many forms of algae.

▼ In the aquarium, the yellow sailfin tang grazes on algae, including some Caulerpa and Sargassum species.

* Build up stocking levels over a period of months. Allow for growth and the final size of the species. Leave room to house a species that you may "discover" at a later date.

◀ Most clownfish don't require an anemone in the tank. The aggressive Amphiprion frenatus, or tomato clownfish, is an independent species that does not need an anemone.

Choosing fish (continued)

The dealer will place your chosen fish in plastic bags filled with one-third aquarium water and two-thirds air, or oxygen if the journey is a long one. Placing these bags into brown paper carriers or colored plastic bags enables the fish to travel in the dark to help keep them calm. Stow the bags carefully in your car, and take the fish straight home.

BAGGING UP A FISH

The dealer transfers your chosen fish into a plastic bag partly filled with water. He then adds oxygen (left) and knots the bag tightly (above). Finally, the fish are placed into dark surroundings (right) for a less stressful journey home.

INTRODUCING THE FISH

1 Equalize the transport water with that in the aquarium by floating the unopened bags in the tank, preferably with the lights off, for about 15 minutes. Then open the bags, and roll down the tops.

2 Before releasing the fish, drip some water from the main aquarium into the bag. This avoids adding high-nitrate water (often found in dealers' aquariums) into the home aquarium.

COPING WITH BULLYING

Slightly reorganizing the tank decor before adding new fish can help prevent territorial squabbles, but sometimes a bullying problem occurs after you add a new fish to the tank. The new fish can be either the aggressor or the victim. If the situation does not improve, you can try various options. One is to cover the aquarium with a heavy blanket for forty-eight hours. Theoretically, during this period of enforced darkness, the newcomer will be readily accepted or the bully will calm down. Another strategy is to place a clear plastic divider in the tank for up to two weeks to separate the dominant bully from the rest of the fish. A further step is to transfer the aggressor to another tank for a week or two to allow the new fish to settle into the display aquarium, but this could stress the bully and disrupt its feeding pattern. Ultimately, you may have to return the bully to the dealer, or if the victim is a single fish, return the victim instead.

If your aquarium is normally left open, it is a good idea to keep it covered for the first few nights after introducing new fish. Many fish have a tendency to jump at night if they are spooked by other tank inhabitants. Once they have found a refuge, they will settle down.

▲ Cowfish are liable to produce a lethal toxin if stressed during transportation. Transport the fish separately (and singly) as any toxin they produce will kill them and everything else in the bag, too.

◀ Many popular marine fish are extremely long lived. Clownfish can live to be well over twelve years of age, and some species of true angel, such as the French angel (Pomacanthus paru) shown left, can live for more than twenty years in captivity.

CHOOSING FISH

What are invertebrates?

The term *invertebrate* loosely covers all those animals that do not have a backbone, or vertebral column, and an internal skeleton. A wide range of invertebrate life can be kept in captivity; suitable species include mollusks, shrimps, crabs, sea anemones, soft and stony corals, starfish, and tube worms. A piece of live rock may have tiny polyps or fanworms living on it. Many invertebrates coexist with fish; indeed, many fish and invertebrates have close associations in nature.

INVERTEBRATE HERBIVORES

Invertebrate herbivores help to control problem algae. The usual herbivores to start off with are "turbo" snails (mollusks) and hermit crabs (crustaceans). *Turbo snail* describes any of a number of snail species, all with a conical shell. The two most popular hermit crabs are red legs and blue legs. Hermit crabs need a supply of new shells of progressively larger size to move into as they grow.

▲ *Turbo snails are a valuable addition to a reef system. Buy a mix of species, such as* Astraea, Trochus, *and* Turbo.

* *Do not be alarmed if you see what looks like the dead body of a hermit crab soon after introduction. It is probably a discarded molt.*

◀ *Hermit crabs can be very entertaining as they try on new shells and return them if they do not "fit."*

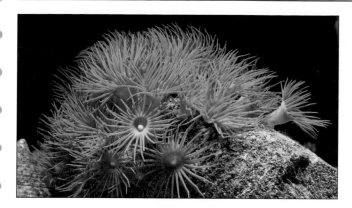

◀ *Zoanthid yellow polyps are a good first choice of coral, being hardy, colorful, and inexpensive. Although it is a photosynthetic coral, it does not depend on really bright light.*

BUYING CORALS

Corals are packed in the same way as fish, although they should be double-bagged to prevent the weight of the rock and water from puncturing the bags. In the shop, make sure your coral is bagged under water so that air is not trapped in any areas of the coral, which will lead to the tissue in that area dying. Bagging under water also helps to preserve any sponges that may be attached to the rock.

* "Frags" are a cheaper way of buying corals. They are fragments of coral that have been fixed to rocks, usually using epoxy glue, and grown in a coral nursery until they are of marketable size.

▶ *This toadstool coral* (Sarcophyton) *is one of several soft corals suitable for the marine aquarium. Others include cabbage/finger* (Sinularia), *colt/pussey* (Alcyonium), *and cauliflower coral* (Cladiella).

Compatibility

Compatibility is of the utmost importance, particularly when setting up a reef aquarium. The aim is to create a harmonious environment, with none of the inhabitants preying on one another. Compatibility problems are not limited to fish. When invertebrates are added to the mix in a reef aquarium, there is a whole new set of compatibility issues to consider. Many fish will quite happily devour small invertebrates as part of their omnivorous diet. Occasionally, the reverse is true; some invertebrates, including mantis shrimps, swimming crabs, and *Cerianthus* sea anemones, will prey upon fish. Giant mushroom polyps or large hermit crabs have been known to take unsuspecting fish.

GET ADVICE

If have any doubt about compatibility issues with a particular fish, consult your dealer before you buy. Take a list of the fish and other species in your aquarium, and ask whether the fish you are considering is a suitable addition.

▼ *The raccoon butterflyfish* (Chaetodon lunula) *eats anemones and polyps. It may even eat smaller ornamental shrimp.*

▲ *If a fish is known to exhibit particularly territorial behavior, such as the striped damsel* (Dascyllus aruanus), *introduce it last; otherwise, it could mercilessly attack any newcomers introduced after it.*

▼ *Carpet anemones* (Stichodactyla gigantea) *have densely packed tentacles with a powerful sting. They are capable of capturing fish and mobile invertebrates.*

◀ Compatibility can also mean keeping species together. Some fish team up for foraging purposes. For example, wrasse species (here, moon wrasse) often follow triggerfish and parrot fish, which may flush out tiny invertebrates that the smaller fish can eat.

▶ If you plan to introduce two closely related and territorial species, such as the yellow sailfin tang (Zebrasoma flavescens) and the purple tang (Z. xanthurum), first put in a small individual of one species, then a smaller fish of the second species, unless you can add both simultaneously.

* Tension and aggression will be heightened between fish of a similar size and body shape or with a similar pattern. The more closely two fish are related, the greater the chance of disputes.

A NATURAL WAR ZONE

Natural reefs are a war zone. Species of coral compete for the available substrate by chemical warfare, overwhelming their "enemies" through fast growth and by physically stinging them to death. Allow for ample growth when positioning corals.

▼ Bear in mind that there is a difference between invertebrate compatibility and coral compatibility. For example, dottybacks (Pseudochromis spp.) will not harm corals but can present a threat to ornamental shrimp.

COMPATIBILITY

The completed aquarium

This is the finished aquarium from the sequence started on page 22, including the initial livestock. Introduce only one fish or invertebrate at a time unless they are small enough to allow more. Always monitor the water quality before making any further introductions to avoid overburdening the filter system and, in turn, stressing the animals.

In addition to playing an important role in water quality control, the living rock habitat not only supports its own community of living organisms but also provides retreats for other aquarium subjects and is a base for adding live corals, anemones, and other sessile creatures.

The yellow sailfin tang (*Zebrasoma flavescens*) is a hardy fish ideally suited to this type of aquarium setup.

Skunk cleaner shrimps (*Lysmata amboinensis*) often perch on rocks advertising their services.

MARINE MACROALGAE

There are many beautiful species of marine algae that if kept in check, can enhance the appearance of a marine aquarium. However, many are prone to rapid die-off, resulting in the release of a large quantity of nutrients into the aquarium. Regular thinning, rather than occasional heavy pruning, is the best way to keep growth under control. Herbivorous fish such as tangs (*Zebrasoma* spp) are useful in controlling macroalgae growth.

▲ Halimeda *sp. is a beautiful alga with a calcareous "skeleton" that often appears spontaneously from live rock or coral base rock.*

▲ *Caulerpa prolifera grows rapidly. Many species of Caulerpa are banned in some areas of the United States.*

▲ *Grape alga* (Caulerpa racemosa) *has a deserved reputation for accelerated growth and is banned in California.*

◀ *The red alga Halymenia sp. is common on live rock and will thrive in nutrient-rich water. It's ideal for a beginner's algae tank, but it will vanish in tanks poor in nitrate and phosphate.*

THE COMPLETED AQUARIUM

A reef aquarium

On these pages, we follow the process of setting up a 7.5-ft- (2.3-m-) long reef aquarium with a capacity of approximately 300 gallons (1,130 liters). It features high-flow water circulation with a large sump (incorporating a deep sand bed), a refugium, and high-intensity lighting for optimal coral growth. This sizable aquarium will accommodate larger fish species as well as provide space for interesting rock architecture.

1 The base cabinet houses the deep sand bed and refugium above it. The cabinet has a steel frame at the back to support the weight of the main tank.

This part of the sump provides a large freshwater top-off tank.

2 The main tank was built in situ. The glass base was drilled for water overflow via a weir into the sump and for water returns via closed loops. Very clear, low-iron glass was used for the front and sides.

3 The cabinet houses a protein skimmer (front) and calcium reactor. The skimmer is fed by water from a spur off the main return pump and the reactor by a peristaltic pump from the refugium. Both return water via the sump.

* Asynchronous pumps generate a pulsed water flow to simulate conditions on a typical coral reef.

A REEF AQUARIUM

THE NEXT STAGES IN CONSTRUCTION

4 The main tank was checked for leaks by running the system with tap water. The closed loop pipes return water at low, middle, and high levels for maximal circulation. The overflow weir was placed centrally in the tank in order to collect surface water evenly.

5 The tank was filled with salt water and the sand bed added. The sand was allowed to settle, and then the live rock added. During this time, the water was heated and recirculated via the main pump with the protein skimmer operational. The system was left to mature in this state for several weeks. Nitrite and nitrate levels were checked regularly during this period to monitor the maturing process.

6 Three sequence pumps are used to circulate the water; one for the main return pump and two for the closed loops. All are fed from the weir. These are located outside in a weatherproof cabinet to reduce noise in the tank room. A hole was therefore made in the wall of the house to accommodate the necessary pipes.

7 Some snails were added one to two weeks after the live rock not only to control the inevitable algal growth but also to maintain the necessary beneficial denitrifying bacteria.

* The deep sand bed was added to a depth of 6 in (15 cm) about two weeks before the live rock, and it was topped with live coral sand.

8 The tank water cleared, and signs of life appeared around the rocks, including tube worms and microfauna (amphipods, copepods). This confirmed that the tank was maturing properly. The rocks were arranged into their final positions to hide the pipes where possible.

A reef aquarium (continued)

9 Corals were added and the main lights switched on. It was important to consider the growth patterns of the corals and their requirements for light and water flow. Corals may attack or shade each other as they grow. The fish were added one at a time with at least one month's interval between additions to minimize the bioburden and stress to the fish. After eleven months, there were clear signs of good coral growth.

10 After thirty months, the corals had attained a mature size (particularly the plating *Montipora* coral) and were beginning to encroach on each other. Careful gardening was required to minimize the risk of the corals attacking each other.

* A computer controls and monitors the tank's parameters, including lighting intervals, temperature, pH, conductivity, water flow, water level, and calcium reactor.

Compare the size of this blue *Acropora* coral with its growth after a further nineteen months — Step 10.

11 The frogspawn coral (*Euphyllia* sp.) has grown very large and consists of more than forty individual heads.

12 A large clam sits under the partial shadow of an orange *Montipora* coral. Shadows produced by the spreading corals, such as the blue table *Acropora*, can also provide refuge for fish at night when the lights are switched off.

Feeding

Nutrition has a direct impact on the appearance, color, growth rate, disease resistance, reproductivity, and general well-being of your fish and invertebrates. Their diet must provide the essential components of proteins, fats, carbohydrates, minerals, and vitamins. Use a variety of foods to meet these needs. Frozen foods are by far the most popular and appropriate choice for most reef fish. There is a good range available, including foods formulated for difficult feeders, foods enriched with HUFAs (highly unsaturated fatty acids), and foods that have been irradiated to ensure they are parasite free.

DEFROSTED FROZEN FOODS

Whole cockle
Accepted by many
marine fish

Marine mix
Natural marine
invertebrate and
fish meats

Krill
Nutritious food for
larger fish; break up for
small fish

Small fish
A "one-gulp food"
for larger fish

Shrimp
Many wild-caught
foods are irradiated.

* Do not use fish food aimed at the freshwater or cold-water market, as it may contain too much fat. Marine fish need a high-protein (40–60%) but relatively low-fat (5–10%) diet to thrive.

Frozen foods are sold in single slabs. Break off pieces as required.

Allow frozen foods to thaw before feeding them to prevent the fish from eating ice.

▼ Mysis shrimp are a much better "staple" as they contain a greater percentage of fat, which helps to keep weight on fish that might become emaciated if fed solely on brine shrimp.

▲ Brine shrimp are a useful first food for most marine fish, but many species will need far more nourishment than brine shrimp can provide, even if enriched.

FLAKE AND GRANULAR FOODS

High-quality mixed flake formulations contain many of the vitamins and proteins required by the majority of marine fish.

Brine shrimp in flake form

Fast-sinking granular foods help to ensure that bottom-feeding fish receive a supply of food.

DRIED MARINE SEAWEED

Herbivores in the reef should have food available all the time. They need to be constantly browsing. Supplement the algae naturally available in your reef with dried marine seaweeds (macroalgae). You can fit a sheet in a sucker-mounted clip or between the two halves of a magnetic algae scraper. This way, the fish know where to find it, and it won't drift around the aquarium to be sucked into the filter.

▶ Many varieties of macroalgae are available, which is just as well as some tangs have the habit of settling on one type to the exclusion of all others.

Feeding (continued)

Provide your fish with a varied diet to prevent them from becoming too set in their ways. Although modern prepared foods contain all the necessary nutrients and vitamins, even the slight differences between various manufacturers' mixes will provide an appetizing change for them. When buying frozen foods, buy a different type each week to build up a good range, and then feed in rotation.

◀ *Live phytoplankton is nonpolluting. The primary users are the minor animals that go on to feed corals and fish by reproducing and providing edible plankton (eggs, sperm, and larvae) or by being eaten themselves.*

▲ *Puffer fish and porcupine fish have formidable teeth, fused into a beaklike structure. These grow continuously. Provide hard-shelled foods, such as frozen whole shrimp and cockle in the shell, to enable these fish to keep their teeth short.*

* Light is food for algae and also for the zooxanthellae harbored by corals. Make sure yo have appropriate levels of light to maintain the animals and plants you wish to keep.

TARGET FEEDING

A good method of feeding corals is to mix frozen foods of appropriate size with phytoplankton in a measure of tank water. Stir this until the frozen food has defrosted, and "target-feed" the corals using a turkey baster. Gently direct a stream of food at individual corals until you see them capturing it.

◀ *Persuading predators such as this Fu Manchu lionfish (Dendrochirus biocellatus) to accept dead foods can be difficult. Buy fish that are feeding well.*

FEEDING

◀ Feed fish little and often. Net out any food that remains uneaten after two to three minutes. Try to feed in the morning, late afternoon, and just before the lights go out. The morning and night feeds are the most important.

▶ Unlike fish, sessile invertebrates cannot chase after food; it has to be delivered to them. Turn off filtration systems for a short period while feeding invertebrates with liquid food; otherwise, the filter will "eat" the food before the inverts do.

* Before acquiring any fish species, familiarize yourself with their feeding requirements, and be sure that you can meet them.

◀ Ensure that all the fish get their share at feeding time. Stock the aquarium carefully to ensure that voracious feeders are not kept with delicate species. Some fish become more active at night, so make sure that food is available for such species during the hours of darkness.

Maintaining the aquarium

Biological changes will occur in the aquarium as it matures. However efficient it may be, a filtration system cannot degrade all the waste products generated by the inhabitants. Organic compounds tend to accumulate in the water, as will nitrate in many tanks. A tendency toward a falling pH level is a natural trend, and trace elements become exhausted over time. The simple process of regular (weekly) partial water changes is the solution to many of these problems.

PARTIAL WATER CHANGES

If there are no apparent algae problems, simply siphon out the water into a bucket using a length of 0.5 in (12 mm) flexible hose. If there is a biofilm on the water surface, scoop it off. If there is an algae problem, try siphoning with a length of airline. This slows down the rate at which you take water from the tank, allowing you time to siphon out the pest algae. Never mix new supplies of salt water directly in the aquarium; use a food-safe plastic bucket, and ideally mix the new water at least two to three days before adding it to the aquarium. This will ensure that the salt has fully dissolved. Check the salinity of newly made water before

Direct the water from the tank into a bucket on the ground.

adding it to the tank and again fifteen minutes after it has been introduced. If the salinity is too high, slowly add RO water, about one quart (liter) at a time. If it is too low, mix a small amount of water at a higher salinity and add that. Occasionally, it may be necessary to top off because of evaporation loss. As only water evaporates, leaving the salts behind, you must top off with fresh water.

TESTING pH LEVEL

◀ *Check the pH level weekly, making sure it remains stable at around 8.3 but no higher— and no lower than 8.1. Also take a weekly salinity reading.*

TESTING FOR AMMONIA

◀ *Test ammonia (here) and nitrite levels every two weeks. Both should be zero. It is also a good idea to check nitrate levels; aim for levels below 5 mg per quart (liter).*

CLEANING FILTER MEDIA

In a fish-only system, monitor the rate of water flow returning from any external canister filter. If it slows down, the filter needs cleaning. Do not change or rinse out and reuse the entire medium at once. Changing a proportion at a time (using aquarium water to rinse it out) helps to retain the colony of nitrifying bacteria.

▲ *Rinse out filter media in aquarium water to retain the beneficial bacteria.*

◀ *Any buildup of dirt or algae inside the reaction chamber of the protein skimmer (rather than the inside of the collecting cup) may adversely affect the skimmer's efficiency. In a heavily loaded system, the protein skimmer may need cleaning once or twice a week. This one is working efficiently.*

* *Carry out a daily visual check on the tank. Monitor the behavior, apparent health, and number of your livestock. Check the operation of filters, protein skimmers, powerheads, heaters, and air stones. Remove uneaten food and dead livestock.*

▲ *Change lamps on a regular basis. As a rough guide, replace all fluorescent tubes every twelve months, and actinic lamps every six months.*

MAINTAINING THE AQUARIUM

Maintaining the aquarium (continued)

A reef aquarium poses additional maintenance considerations. Calcium can be deposited in such a way as to impair the operation of mechanical equipment. Invertebrates such as snails, sponges, and crustaceans can block pipes, leading to flooding and other problems. Clean and service all equipment on a regular basis.

CALCIUM AND CARBONATE

As the number of animals in the reef increases, water changes will no longer be enough to supply their calcium and carbonate demand. For the smaller tank or one with a lower demand, choose one of the balanced, two-part additives on sale. With larger tanks or those with a high demand, it may be more economical to use a calcium reactor or device that automatically mixes kalkwasser. Carbonate and calcium levels are inextricably linked. You can monitor carbonate levels with the knowledge that if these change, it is time to check the calcium levels.

A Counting each drop, add KH reagent a drop at a time to a 5 ml sample of tank water. Swirl the tube.
B Initially, the sample turns blue.
C As more reagent is added, the sample turns yellow. Continue counting the drops added until the yellow color is stable. Each drop added from the beginning of the test represents 1°dH, equivalent to 17.5 mg per quart (liter) of carbonate.

A   B   C

A CALCIUM REACTOR

◀ *A calcium reactor passes tank water through a calcareous medium while adding CO_2 to the reactor. This acidifies the water, dissolving calcium and carbonates in a balanced manner, making them available to the corals.*

* *Some salts contain enhanced levels of calcium and carbonate. Using these mixes may delay the need for supplementation, but they should not be relied on to maintain the proper levels.*

A KALKWASSER STIRRER

◀ *A kalkwasser stirrer mixes calcium hydroxide into RO water, which is then used to top off the tank, thus replenishing calcium while making up for evaporation losses. Calcium hydroxide has a very high pH, which is potentially dangerous to the tank inhabitants as well as to humans and other animals. Treat it with care.*

▲ *This "frag" of Acropora coral needs calcium to develop its stony structure.*

PHOSPHATE TEST

▲ *Add phosphate reagent to a sample of tank water and mix. After five minutes, look down the tube to compare the color of the solution with the chart.*

* As well as testing for undesirable elements, such as ammonia and nitrite, and test kits tell you what of good components are missing in the water, such as oxygen, iodine, and calcium.

USING WATER TESTS

Always follow the manufacturer's instructions carefully when testing water parameters; not all test kits use the same technique, especially when it comes to comparing the colors of the test vial against the supplied color chart. Keep a check on the "best before" date of the reagents. Liquid reagents age more quickly than dry

▲ *Regular water testing is vital.*

ones, which can produce misleading results. The shelf life of some reagents is as short as six months, so don't skimp on your testing; make the most of your test kits!

Health care

One of the best ways to ensure the good health of your charges, both fish and invertebrates, is to maintain good-quality, stable water conditions and a stress-free environment. Most health problems come down to environmental problems, such as equipment failure or malfunction, or aquarist-induced problems, such as inattention or lack of knowledge. One obvious way to prevent disease is to quarantine all fish and invertebrates before adding them to the display tank.

A QUARANTINE TANK

Use a to maintain water temperature.

Fit a guard to protect fish that might rest against the heater element.

Use a small (18—24 gallon [68—90-liter] clean tank with no substrate.

The quarantine tank can be sparsely furnished.

Slate is an inert material and will not affect the water quality.

Small internal power filter with sponge medium

A clay flowerpot provides a useful hiding place.

WHY QUARANTINE?

In a reef system, it is virtually impossible to catch fish established in rocks. An infected fish can easily pass on disease organisms to other fish, and given the difficulty of treating fish disease in a reef setting, this can easily lead to a fish wipe-out. That is why quarantining new fish is vital. The recommended quarantine period for fish is usually fourteen to twenty-one days. Quarantining invertebrates for seven to fourteen days helps you avoid introducing potential pest organisms.

▲ *It is not possible to treat fish in the aquarium with copper-based remedies if invertebrates are also present. Although the fish respond well, invertebrates cannot tolerate copper at all and will be killed. A few proprietary remedies are safe to use with invertebrates, but these are far less effective than copper. If an infection is severe, it may be best to catch the infected fish and treat it in a separate tank.*

HEALTH CARE

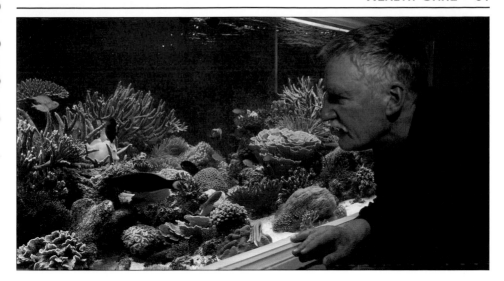

HEALTH CARE

▲ *Observe your fish on a regular basis, as the first signs of disease are often behavioral changes. Fish may sulk in the corner of the tank, look off-color, or refuse to feed. Persistent scratching is a sign of irritation, probably parasitic. More obvious signs of disease are ragged fins, inflamed gills, and ulceration or spots on the fins, body, or gills.*

* If you suspect a problem, first check the aquarium conditions, especially water parameters. Consult reference sources, ask for advice, and do not rush into inappropriate or unnecessary treatment.

FRESHWATER BATHS

A two- to three-minute freshwater bath can be used as a prophylactic treatment for new fish additions. Any parasites will rupture under the osmotic shock of fresh water long before the fish experiences any harmful effects. The fresh water must be at the same temperature and pH as your tank water. The same treatment can be used to rid corals of predatory nudibranchs and flatworms.

▼ *In the confines of an aquarium, a parasite such as white spot (Cryptocaryon irritans) can complete its life cycle quickly and multiply at a tremendous rate, thus overwhelming the original carrier fish and passing it quickly to its tank mates.*

Health care (continued)

When using a medication, read the instructions! Some medications may not be suitable for certain fish species. Remove activated carbon media from the filtration system during treatment, as it will remove the medication before a cure is effected. Many medications also require you to suspend protein skimming for the duration of the treatment.

USING MEDICATIONS

If a treatment fails to work, never add another medication right away. Return the water conditions in the treatment tank to normal before trying another remedy. After successful treatment, always restore the water conditions in the treatment tank to those of the main aquarium before returning the patient.

▼ *Accurate dosing is essential, so it helps to know the exact volume of water in your aquarium. Premix medication in a little tank water before adding it to the treatment tank.*

COMMON PROBLEMS

White spot A covering of tiny white spots on the body and fins caused by the parasite *Cryptocaryon irritans*. Treat it with copper-based medication.

Velvet Fine, white dusting on the skin, giving a velvety appearance. The gills may also be affected. Fish often dash around, breathing rapidly. It is caused by *Amyloodinium*. Treat it with copper-based medication.

Lymphocystis Fine, cauliflowerlike growths on fins and skin. There is no direct cure. Ozone or UV may reduce its spread. It may heal on its own in otherwise healthy fish.

Brooklynella hostilis This protozoan parasite causes turbidity of the skin. This is common in clownfish and leads to shedding of copious amounts of mucus. The infestation does not respond to copper treatments and is usually associated with poor water conditions, either in the aquarium or during shipping.

UV STERILIZATION

UV sterilization is a very useful, noninvasive way of dealing with a number of diseases in both the fish-only and the reef aquarium. Fish-only systems may do better with the continuous use of UV sterilization, taking into account the higher stocking levels. In a sensibly stocked reef system, fish should be at lower risk of stress-induced disease, and it is probably sufficient to run UV sterilization for two to three weeks when adding new fish. Run the UV when you detect the presence of disease, and continue to do so, again for two to three weeks, after the last symptoms of disease have disappeared.

Water flows through this outer glass tube.

The aquarium water can be sterilized by passing it through a UV unit.

This quartz sleeve encases the tube but allows UV light to pass through.

The fluorescent tube in the middle produces ultraviolet light, which is harmful to living tissue.

* Clean and sterilize the treatment tank and all associated equipment after each and every use. To sterilize, use either proprietary aquarium products or those available for treating baby bottles. Rinse well with fresh water, and leave to dry.

HUMANE DISPATCH

If all else fails and you have to dispose of a fish humanely, the best option is to obtain the anaesthetic MS222 from a veterinarian. Follow the instructions closely, and leave the fish in the solution for a few hours.

Breeding

Breeding marine fish is one of the most rewarding aspects of the hobby, and every aquarist should attempt it at least once. Many marine fish will spawn in a reef aquarium. If you are serious about raising the larvae, you may have to remove the adult breeding pair to a separate aquarium, where you can observe the potential parents and monitor egg development more easily. The most commonly raised marine fish species are Banggai cardinals and clownfish. Damselfish species such as gold chromis, neon gobies, and various dottyback species also breed readily.

— A juvenile Banggai cardinalfish

◀ *The female Banggai cardinalfish lays a ball of eggs that the male takes into his mouth for incubation. When they emerge, the young are highly developed and large enough to accept newly hatched brine shrimp and frozen foods of appropriate size. (See also page 61.)*

FEEDING LARVAE

To survive, marine fish larvae first require live foods in the form of rotifers, followed by newly hatched brine shrimp and, finally, dried foods. Feed the rotifers on phytoplankton to keep them alive and reproducing. Keep up the rotifer density and that of the phytoplankton; otherwise, the larvae will starve. After five to ten days, depending on species, move on to the brine shrimp, but continue to offer rotifers for the smaller larvae.

Be sure to have food cultures up and running before there are any larvae to raise. Introduce dry foods early, starting with powdered flake and gradually increasing the food particle size as required. Try feeding new foods first thing in the morning when the larvae are hungry. To avoid the risk of water pollution, be sure to clean out all uneaten food, and minimize the amount you introduce until you are sure it is being eaten.

A CLOWNFISH BREEDING TANK

A simple bubble-up sponge filter

Tank measuring 30x12x15 in (75x30x38 cm).

Provide a flat surface, such as a piece of slate, for the fish to lay their eggs on.

◀ *Clownfish should lay their eggs on a cleaned, flat surface. The evening before hatching is due, transfer the eggs to a separate rearing tank, where you can attempt to raise the larvae free of the risk of predation.*

An anemone is a nice addition, but most are difficult to maintain.

A LARVAL-RAISING TANK

Flexible air line connected to rigid air line

Heaterstat

Tank measuring 24 × 12 × 12. in (60 × 30 × 30 cm)

Dark material to shade the back and sides from light

Fill the tank halfway with water from the parental system.

Thermometer

Ammonia alert badge

Air pump

Polystyrene base

▲ *Set up the tank as shown here. Prepare a black cover for the front glass. Regulate the airflow to provide good water circulation without excessively vigorous bubbling. Ensure that the heater is covered by water. Adjust it over a period of twenty-four hours to maintain a temperature of 80°F (27°C). Provide a photoperiod of twelve to sixteen hours using standard T8 fluorescent lights.*

* *Blacking out the tank makes it easier for the larvae to see their prey and prevents them from being distracted by light outside the tank. After five to seven days, when the larvae's eyes have developed a little more, discard the front cover.*

Breeding (continued)

To encourage any aquatic animal to breed, you must first provide good water quality, followed by a compatible mate, a safe environment, and good nutrition. Some species may have further requirements, such as cues relating to the lunar cycle or changes in salinity or temperature that stimulate breeding. Always find out as much as you can before attempting to breed any marine fish or invertebrate species.

◀ *Although the female sea horse produces the eggs, she transfers them to the male's pouch, where they develop until they are ready to emerge as miniature versions of their parents. Captive-bred sea horses often require live brine shrimp to begin with but can be gradually weaned onto frozen foods, such as chopped mysis shrimp, which is more nutritious.*

▶ *Most of the invertebrates that reproduce in the aquarium do so by asexual means, whereby the foot of an anemone or polyp splits, producing two daughter colonies from the parent colony. Baby colonies form directly on the stem of soft corals such as* Sarcophyton sp.

◀ *Two Lysmata shrimps of the same species (here L. amboinensis) constitute a pair. Both will carry eggs on a regular basis, usually releasing larvae late at night. Raise them in a setup as described on page 55. Be sure to prevent the buildup of hair algae in which the tiny shrimps could become caught. While shrimps are growing and molting, they remain free swimming. After the final molt, the larvae become true juvenile shrimps and substrate orientated, venturing into the water column only when food is introduced.*

MARINE LIVESTOCK

The sheer variety of suitable marine fish to choose from is one of the main reasons for the hobby's popularity. The most striking tropical marine fish are native to coral reefs and coastal waters, where collection is quite easy. Fish from the deepest waters usually grow too large for the aquarium and also present too many collection and transportation problems. The majority of suitable fish come from the Indo-Pacific oceans, the Caribbean area of the Northern Atlantic Ocean, and the Red Sea.

When you go to buy your fish and invertebrates, bear in mind that within every family there are anomalies. Not all species in a particular family may be suitable for aquarium life, so always research your chosen species, and seek advice from your aquatic dealer. When requesting information about a particular species from a dealer, it is helpful to know the scientific (Latin) name to avoid any potential confusion. Certain species will have several common names but only one scientific name. It may seem like a bit of a mouthful, but it could prevent you from buying the wrong fish. When buying fish, take accurate information with you about the size of your tank and the existing inhabitants.

On the following pages, you will find an introduction to some of the fish and invertebrates found in each of the families commonly available in aquatic shops. Some are relatively hardy and easy to care for, whereas others may have specific dietary requirements or behavioral traits that you must take into consideration before buying. Many popular marine fish are extremely long lived, so the choices you make when you first stock your aquarium are very important, as you may well be sharing your living space with these fish for many years to come.

Clownfish

Clownfish (anemonefish) are hardy, relatively inexpensive, and readily available. Some are long lived. They will accept most foods, achieve a modest maximum size, and usually tolerate other individuals of the same size. Given good care, they are likely to breed in the aquarium. In common with damselfish and cardinalfish, they use invertebrates for protection; in fact, the sight of a common clownfish among the tentacles of its host anemone is one that first attracts many fishkeepers to the marine hobby.

◀ *The body color of Clarke's clownfish* (Amphiprion clarkii) *ranges from light brown to jet black. At 6 in (15 cm) maximum size, females are larger than males (4 in [10 cm]) maximum). A large fish can be quite belligerent toward anything that threatens its anemone.*

The fiery coloration of small individuals becomes more subdued with time.

The tomato clownfish can be distinguished from closely related species by the black leading edge of the pelvic fins.

* Clownfish are known to inhabit any one of nine species of host anemone. Clarke's clownfish is the only species to occupy all nine. However, maintaining anemones in aquariums is challenging and best left to experienced aquarists.

▲ *The tomato clownfish* (Amphiprion frenatus) *is another powerful species (females 5.5 in [14 cm], males a little smaller) that is prepared to defend its host anemone vigorously. It does well with the bubbletip anemone* (Entacmaea quadricolor).

▶ *Once settled, the instantly recognizable and hugely popular common clownfish* (Amphiprion ocellaris) *accepts a range of live and dried aquarium foods.*

* The common clownfish is one of the most popular fish raised in captivity. Given the availability of beautifully marked, healthy captive-bred specimens, it is hard to justify large-scale collection of this species from the wild.

Body color is variable, ranging from pale yellow to red-orange.

◀ *Although very similar to* A. ocellaris, *the percula clownfish (*A. percula*) has more black pigment on the body.*

Many species of clownfish can have incomplete vertical bands.

Its larger size (females up to 7 in [17 cm]), deep coloration, and three white stripes make the maroon clownfish easy to identify.

▶ *Do not keep the maroon clownfish (*Premnas biaculeatus*) with other clownfish. It will dominate an aquarium, particularly when living with a host anemone. In the wild, it exclusively inhabits the bubbletip anemone, but in the aquarium, it can fend for itself without an anemone.*

Damsels and Cardinals

Damselfish are closely related to clownfish. While generally easy to care for, they may squabble among themselves, so provide an aquarium large enough to give each fish a reasonable amount of territory. Cardinalfish are much less active than damsels or clownfish and may even be nocturnal. Juvenile cardinals of many species live close to or in anemones but also use other invertebrates, such as sea urchins, for protection.

Males grow to a maximum size of 3 in (8 cm); females are smaller.

◀ *The undemanding blue-green chromis* (Chromis viridis) *is a small, shoaling damselfish, so keep it in a group of three or more. It will breed in the aquarium, where males dominate harems of females and vigorously guard the nest site.*

▶ *It is often possible to house a group of Fijian blue and gold damselfish* (Chrysiptera taupou) *in the aquarium, as long as the fish are stocked simultaneously and at a small size.*

▼ *Keep the Andaman damselfish* (Pomacentrus alleni) *with peaceful species that will not constantly chase it. It is not as robust as other damsels, and if stressed, it will not leave the refuge of the rock.*

The male fish has a black edge to the front part of the dorsal fin. In females, this region is yellow.

* The Andaman damselfish can turn its incredible color and patterning on and off at will. This appears to be the result of a pecking order, whereby dominant individuals earn the right to display their full beauty.

◀ *The striking Banggai cardinalfish is one of the easiest marine fish to breed and raise in captivity. Try to obtain male-female pairs; otherwise, fighting can occur. The fish can be kept in shoals in a sufficiently large aquarium.*

Mature males have a more massive jaw structure.

BREEDING THE BANGGAI

Once the female has deposited eggs in the form of a cluster or ball, they are taken into the mouth of the male for incubation. Even after hatching, the juvenile fish remain in the mouth for protection from predators. When they emerge—as tiny, fully formed replicas of the adults—juveniles immediately seek out the protection of the long-spined sea urchin (*Diadema* sp.), with which they associate in the wild. It is not essential to keep sea urchins in order to rear this species successfully, but if they are not available, separate the juveniles from the adults, at least until they have grown larger. Some aquarists use artificial urchins with good results. Juvenile Banggai cardinals will sometimes protect themselves in anemones if urchins are not present in the aquarium. Feed the young as described on pages 54–55.

* During much of the day, the pyjama cardinalfish hides among the branches of stony corals. It becomes much more active at night or under blue actinic lights.

▶ *The benign behavior and attractive coloration of the pyjama cardinalfish (Sphaeramia nematoptera) make it a popular choice with marine aquarists.*

The body is quite stocky and deep. Males are generally larger and have larger mouths.

Dwarf angelfish

Most dwarf angelfish (genus *Centropyge*) remain fairly small (less than 6 in [15 cm]). They are attractive, colorful, and active and a favorite of aquarists, particularly those with reef aquariums, even though they can never be fully trusted not to nip at invertebrates.

Good specimens appear bright eyed and have a uniform blue body color.

◀ *The cherub, or pygmy, angelfish (Centropyge argi) is the smallest of the dwarf angels; males measure 3 in (8 cm), females 2.5 in (6 cm).*

▶ *Bicolor dwarf angelfish (Centropyge bicolor) can be quite shy at first, hiding in the rocks, but become bolder with time.*

Stunning coloration is a major feature. An emaciated fish with slightly faded colors may signify a weak or ailing specimen.

SEXING ANGELFISH

All angelfish are protogynous hermaphrodites, meaning that individuals are female first and become males as they grow larger. Determining sex is therefore difficult, except to say that the largest specimens will be males.

* The natural diet of the bicolor angelfish consists of sponges, tunicates, algae, small worms, and crustaceans. Reproduce this variety in the aquarium, and offer dried algae on which the fish can browse. Add vitamin supplements to frozen formula foods, mysis, and brine shrimp. In time, fish should take flake or granular food.

DWARF ANGELFISH

DWARF ANGELFISH

◀ The coral beauty (Centropyge bispinosa) is one of the most commonly kept marine fish, famed for its beauty and hardiness.

Specimens have varying patterns depending on where they were collected.

* Centropyge dwarf angelfish can be mixed in the aquarium with care. The coral beauty is the most relaxed and therefore least territorial, so if you are considering including this species, plus another couple of dwarf angels, put the coral beauty in first to minimize any conflict.

Keep in a well-established system (more than 12 months old) stocked with plenty of live rock.

▲ The flame dwarf angelfish (Centropyge loricula) is an instantly recognizable, highly desirable, but expensive addition to the marine aquarium. Offer it plenty of grazing material and some of the formula foods designed for dwarf angelfish, plus mysis, brine shrimp, and other meaty foods.

▲ Specimen selection and a varied diet are the keys to long-term success with the small, peaceful, but timid multibanded dwarf angelfish (Centropyge multifasciata).

OTHER POPULAR CENTROPYGE SPECIES

C. aurantia Golden angel
C. eibli Red stripe dwarf angel
C. flavissimus Lemonpeel dwarf angel
C. ferrugatus Rusty dwarf angel
C. heraldi Herald's angel
C. multicolor Multicolor dwarf angel
C. potteri Potter's dwarf angel

True angelfish

True angelfish (family Pomacanthidae) include the genera *Pomacanthus, Apolemichthys, Chaetodontoplus, Pygoplites,* and *Holacanthus*, all medium to large fish, often with personalities to match. They are often available as small juveniles, some with a markedly different appearance to the adult. Given sufficiently good water quality, most settle well into the aquarium, but do not be tempted by beautiful juveniles if you cannot house a large specimen long term.

◀ *Although not the most colorful angelfish, the cream angel (Apolemichthys xanthurus) is one of the cheapest to buy and is easy to maintain in captivity.*

Ensure that a specimen has clear eyes and is feeding well before you buy it.

▼ *The stunning appearance of the adult emperor angelfish (Pomacanthus imperator) makes it an aquarium favorite, but it is an expensive fish to buy.*

▼ *The juvenile is equally attractive but does not resemble the adult in any way. Fish undergoing the transition from juvenile to adult are not particularly appealing.*

* Specialist foods for angelfish are important, but the cream angelfish is also known to take dried algae, mysis, brine shrimp, and chopped shellfish. Given time and a patient aquarist, it may even accept flake and granular foods.

Juveniles are recognized as cleaner fish and therefore not harmed by much larger species.

▼ *Its generally trustworthy behavior and relatively small maximum size (males 9 in [28 cm]), females smaller), make the majestic angelfish* (Pomacanthus navarchus) *the most popular* Pomacanthus *species to be maintained in the reef aquarium.*

ADULT COLORATION

Both *Pomacanthus navarchus* and *P. xanthometapon* (the blueface angel) can undergo metamorphosis to the adult coloration when very small. Fully transformed adults measuring 2.5 in (6 cm) or so are not uncommon and often settle better than larger individuals.

The majestic angelfish lives close to or in rocks. It is prepared to hide for long periods to avoid the attentions of territorial fish.

▶ *The regal angelfish* (Pygoplites diacanthus) *is often the target of bullying by larger tangs and other angels, so it does best when kept as the largest fish in a peaceful aquarium.*

Males and females both grow to 10 in (25 cm).

* In the wild, the regal angelfish feeds on sponges. Provide preparations designed for such species plus frozen foods, vitamin supplements, and nori (a dried seaweed). In time, they may take dried and flake foods.

Red Sea and Indian Ocean specimens have a yellow pelvic region, and these should be the only individuals marine aquarists attempt to keep.

Butterflyfish

The majority of butterflyfish available in the aquarium hobby are members of a single genus, *Chaetodon*, and have a very similar body pattern. Notable exceptions are the genera *Chelmon*, *Forcipiger*, and *Heniochus*, but all require similar care in the home aquarium. Feeding is the major challenge; be sure to investigate the long-term dietary requirements of any species you propose to buy, as some feed only on live coral. Those that include zooplankton as part of their natural diet are some of the easiest to maintain.

C. lunula has a black spot on the caudal peduncle, absent in *C. fasciatus*.

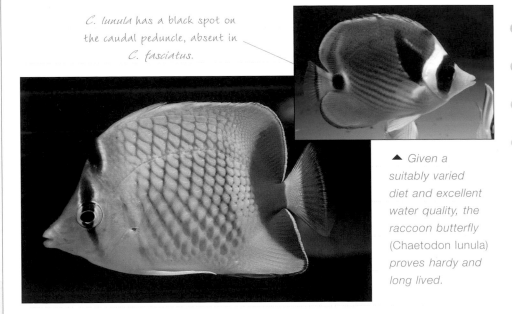

▲ *Given a suitably varied diet and excellent water quality, the raccoon butterfly (Chaetodon lunula) proves hardy and long lived.*

▲ *The Pacific pearlscale (Chaetodon xanthurus) is beautiful and inexpensive. It is one of a group of butterflyfish in which a sector of the rear of the dorsal fin and body is colored orange. Fortunately, all require similar care.*

* The Red Sea raccoon (*Chaetodon fasciatus*) requires similar care to *C. lunula* but is more expensive due to its collection area.

OTHER POPULAR CHAETODON SPECIES

C. argentatus Black pearlscale butterfly
C. auriga Threadfin butterfly
C. burgessi Burgess's butterfly
C. collare Collared butterfly
C. kleini Sunburst butterfly
C. miliaris Milletseed butterflyfish
C. punctatofasciatus Spotband butterfly
C. semilarvatus Masked butterflyfish
C. striatus Banded butterflyfish

▶ *Selecting a fish that is feeding well in the dealer's tank and then offering it a good diet are the keys to success when keeping the copperband butterflyfish* (Chelmon rostratus). *Provide a variety of frozen foods, including shellfish and particularly mysis shrimp, which have a higher fat content than brine shrimp. Feed several times a day and supplement the diet regularly with vitamins.*

* Do not be tempted to introduce the copperband butterflyfish to control the pest anemone species Aiptasia, without giving due consideration to the fish's long-term requirements.

A peaceful species that becomes increasingly confident as it settles into the aquarium.

Given plenty of attention, the copperband can prove hardy and long lived.

◀ *The very long, slender snout of the longnosed butterflyfish* (Forcipiger flavissimus) *enables the fish to remove invertebrates from deep crevices. In the aquarium, it accepts most foods, especially mysis and brine shrimp.*

* If threatened by large surgeonfish and tangs, the longnosed butterflyfish will "headstand," exposing erect dorsal spines in the direction of the threat.

POSSIBLE CONFUSION

Distinguishing between *Forcipiger flavissimus* and the only other species in the genus, *F. longirostris*, is difficult unless you have two specimens side by side. Look for scales with a dark-pigmented center on the thorax of *F. longirostris*.

Wrasses

There are many species of wrasse available, ranging from the large and belligerent to the very small and reclusive. Many hogfish and wrasses show widely varying temperaments among individuals of the same species. Many wrasses show markedly different coloration as they mature, and some are sexually dimorphic (transforming from female to male). The term *hogfish* is generally applied to some of the large wrasse species, most of which grow too large for the home aquarium.

◀ *The stunningly colored Maldive velvet fairy wrasse* (Cirrhilabrus rubrisquamis) *is one of several similar species with the same requirements. Keep it in a peaceful aquarium, and offer enriched brine shrimp, mysis, chopped shellfish, and dried algae. Vitamin supplements help to maintain the vibrant coloration.*

Males are larger and more brightly colored. Females keep their less vivid juvenile coloration.

▼ *The female leopard wrasse* (Macropharyngodon meleagris) *has the leopard markings, while the larger male has orange and green bands on the head, giving way to a deep rusty red body with turquoise spots. This shy species does best in a mature aquarium stocked with plenty of live rock.*

* In common with other species in this group, the Maldive velvet fairy wrasse will sometimes jump out of an uncovered aquarium.

WRASSES

◀ The pyjama wrasse (Pseudocheilinus hexataenia) can prove angelic or demonic, depending on the individual concerned! This small species (males up to 4 in [10 cm]), females and juveniles no more than 2 in [5 cm]) can be kept singly or in male-female pairs.

* Faded colors may indicate that a fish is stressed or has been held in the dealer's tank for some time. After a short period in a home aquarium, the colors become brilliant once more.

▲ The eightline wrasse (Pseudocheilinus octotaenia) may be less striking than its close relative Pseudocheilinus hexataenia but grows larger (5.5 in [14 cm] maximum) and is very hardy in captivity.

▶ The adult coral hogfish (Bodianus mesothorax) looks markedly different from the juvenile, which is jet black with bright yellow spots around the eyes and on the body. The change in coloration occurs quickly at sizes of 2–2.5 in (5–6 cm). Small specimens in adult coloration tend to be hardier and less timid than juveniles.

Male and female coral hogfish grow to 10 in (25 cm). They are sturdy fish with assertive personalities.

WRASSES

Tangs

Tangs from the genera *Zebrasoma* and *Ctenochaetus* are very popular aquarium fish, not only because they are beautiful but also because they play a useful role in the control of nuisance algae. However, these herbivorous fish can be highly territorial, and you must take care when introducing them into an aquarium where some of the more belligerent species are already present.

This subadult has lost the juvenile colors.

◀ With males and females measuring 10 in (25 cm), the chevron tang (Ctenochaetus hawaiiensis) *is the largest species of bristletooth tang. In the wild, the fish use their brushlike teeth to remove fine algal films and detritus from rock surfaces. They are perfectly suited to a reef system.*

The expensive chevron tang is most commonly available as a juvenile.

* Pale specimens may have been in the dealer's tank for some time. They are good buys as they will be settled and well acclimated.

▶ *The beautiful purple tang (Zebrasoma xanthurum) is available in very small sizes, but soon grows larger than Z. flavescens, reaching 10 in (25 cm). In most situations, and regardless of the other species stocked, it will become the dominant fish in any aquarium.*

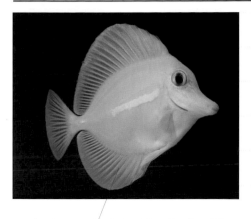

◀ *The popular yellow sailfin tang* (Zebrasoma flavescens) *achieves a moderate maximum size (8.5 in [20 cm]) and aids in preventing unwanted algae.*

This tang is one of the most commonly kept marine species. It is the principal marine fish export from Hawaii.

The behaviour of this species can change from quite submissive when small to belligerent when large.

A SUITABLE DIET

Wild yellow sailfin tangs feed on filamentous algae but graze many different forms of algae in the home aquarium, including some *Caulerpa* and *Sargassum* species. Where there is no algae present, provide dried forms. (Lettuce is a poor substitute for natural marine algae.) Supplement the algae with mysis, brine shrimp, and flaked and pellet foods.

TANGS

◀ *The kole, or yellow-eyed, tang* (Ctenochaetus strigosus) *is an open-water swimmer that often pauses to peck vigorously at the rocks, removing detritus as it does so.*

▶ Ctenochaetus truncatus, *a close relative of* C. strigosus, *also has a gold ring around the eye but white spots on the body, rather than the stripes of* C. strigosus.

Surgeonfish

Surgeonfish possess a pair of modified scales on the caudal peduncle that are scalpel sharp, hence the name surgeonfish. These can be used in attack or defense and are capable of inflicting painful wounds to both aquarists and fish. Members of the genus *Acanthurus* are notoriously territorial; but provided you allow for their growth and are sensible with subsequent stocking, you can enjoy surgeonfish without having to endure their territorial aggression.

▲ *The "scalpel" near the junction of the tail and body shines white here as a warning to predators to keep away.*

The adult coloration is uniformly blue. Juveniles are bright yellow.

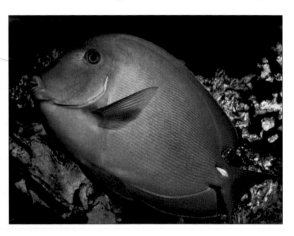

▶ *The Atlantic blue surgeonfish* (Acanthurus coeruleus) *can be highly territorial, severely harassing newly introduced fish. Keep it in a large system (105 gallons [400 liters] or more), and make this fish one of the last larger fish introduced.*

A. pyroferus has more attractive adult coloration than A. tristis (the Indian Ocean mimic surgeonfish).

◀ *If you like the shape and activity of the surgeonfish but cannot stock a fish with aggressive tendencies, the Pacific Ocean mimic surgeonfish* (Acanthurus pyroferus) *is ideal. In the wild, juveniles mimic two, possibly three, angelfish species.*

SURGEONFISH

* Large individuals are capable of moving unsecured pieces of rock or coral base rock as they browse on the algae growing there.

Look for signs of weight loss, which is common in underfed specimens of this active species.

▼ Despite its size (males and females 18 in [45 cm]) and well-developed caudal spines, the orangespine unicornfish (Naso lituratus) is not well able to defend itself against more aggressive species, such as large Acanthurus surgeonfish. It will cohabit with them, but introduce it first to minimize potential problems.

Regal tangs are lively and active unless stressed or threatened, in which case they wedge themselves into any available crevice.

* The regal tang is prone to contracting protozoan parasite infestations shortly after introduction. Offering foods soaked in garlic can help to prevent an outbreak.

▲ The regal tang (Paracanthurus hepatus) is one of the most popular marine fish owing to its striking coloration and availability. To house it long term, keep it in a 130-gallon- (500-liter-) plus aquarium.

Triggers and Puffers

Triggerfish are named for the short, curved dorsal spine that can be used to anchor the fish into rocky crevices from which they cannot be removed unless they intentionally release their locking mechanism. Research the dietary requirements and temperament of any species you propose buying, and do not acquire it unless you have a system capable of holding it for the long term. Species that feed largely on zooplankton in the wild tend to be less aggressive or destructive in the aquarium.

▲ *The clown triggerfish* (Balistoides conspicillum) *is a gorgeous, long-lived, and highly entertaining marine fish. But be aware that it grows rapidly to 18 in (45 cm) and will become quite aggressive—even potentially lethal—toward its tank mates.*

▲ *The Picasso triggerfish* (Rhinecanthus aculeatus) *grows to 12 in (30 cm) and needs a large aquarium; a variety of meaty foods, including shell-on mollusks and crustaceans; and hardy tank mates.*

The Picasso triggerfish is named for its delicate pigment markings.

▼ *Given its natural zooplankton-feeding instincts, the blue throat trigger* (Xanthichthys auromarginatus) *is arguably the triggerfish species most suited for introduction into a reef aquarium.*

Only the male has the blue throat patch and yellow margins to the anal, dorsal, and tail fins.

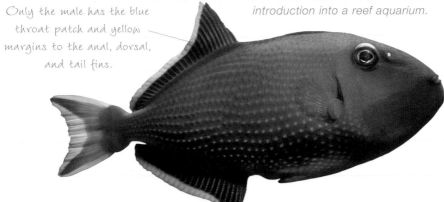

As a defense mechanism, puffer fish and porcupine fish are able to inflate their bodies by sucking in water, which makes them appear larger and more intimidating. In captivity, inflation is seen only in response to an imminent threat or severe stress. *Diodon* species are covered with spines that become erect when they inflate, while other species have skin or internal organs that are toxic.

This puffer fish can be maintained with many other types of fish with few problems but is not reef safe.

▶ The black-spotted puffer fish (Arothron nigropunctatus) *is hardy and long lived and will become quite tame. Provide this omnivore with a varied diet, including dried algae, to satisfy its browsing instincts.*

▼ Its entertaining behavior and bizarre appearance make the porcupine puffer fish (Diodon holocanthus) *a popular choice. Provide meaty foods, preferably in their shells, but bear in mind that this diet puts a heavy demand on the filtration system.*

The porcupine puffer fish is nocturnal and may rest during the day, becoming more active at night. However, as aquarists usually "train" it to receive food during the day, it often becomes more active at this time.

Males and females of this tempting species grow to 18 in (45 cm).

Groupers and Grammas

Although most grouper species are large, predatory fish, they have close relatives that are quite easy to care for long term in the aquarium. Grammas are small, colorful elongate fish; both they and the dottybacks are found close to and among rocks. All can be considered predators, so take care when selecting suitable tank mates, as smaller fish and invertebrates can fall victim to their carnivorous tendencies.

◀ *The comet grouper (Calloplesiops altivelis) has a secretive nature and remains hidden for prolonged periods.*

The golden forktail often swims upside down.

* The comet grouper is also known as the marine betta because its fins resemble those of the freshwater Siamese fighting fish, Betta splendens.

▲ *The golden forktail (Assessor flavissimus), a close relative of the comet grouper, is a peaceful, open-water swimmer and ideal for a reef aquarium.*

POTENTIALLY LARGE

The snowflake, or panther, grouper *(Chromileptes altivelis)* is widely available and instantly recognizable. However, it is a predator that grows slowly but steadily to a considerable size— males 28 in (70 cm), females smaller. Individuals are often on sale at 2–2.5 in (5–6 cm) long, but unless you have a large enough aquarium (minimum 238 gallons [900 liters]), you will have problems later.

▲ *Tank-bred panther groupers may command a higher price than wild fish, but bear in mind that this species is under great pressure in the wild from collectors and fishermen alike.*

* Do not confuse the royal gramma with the similarly colored false gramma, or royal dottyback (*Pseudochromis paccagnellae*), an aggressive species from the Western Pacific.

▲ The stunningly colored and easy-to-keep royal gramma (Gramma loreto) *will thrive in almost any system that does not house more aggressive fish.*

The tiny sunrise dottyback (males 3 in [7 5 cm], females 2.5 in [6.5 cm]), accepts most small meaty foods, including brine shrimp, mysis, and chopped shellfish.

▲ The small but beautifully colored orchid dottyback (Pseudochromis fridmani) *settles well into the aquarium. Pairs spawn frequently. Males guard the eggs laid in caves and may disappear from view at this time.*

▲ Given plenty of rocky cover, a pair of sunrise dottybacks (Pseudochromis flavivertex) *will behave perfectly naturally in the home aquarium.*

PEACEFUL DOTTYBACKS

Red Sea and Arabian Gulf specimens of dottyback (*Pseudochromis spp.*) are often more peaceful than their Indo-Pacific counterparts. They include the orchid dottyback (*P. fridmani*), sunrise (*P. flavivertex*), neon-lined (*P. aldabraensis),* and Sankey's *(P. sankeyi).* The Red Sea species are often available as captive-bred individuals.

Blennies

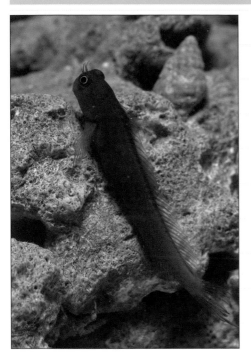

There are many species of peaceful, small blennies to choose from. They can be roughly divided into herbivores and planktivores. Herbivores include *Ecsenius bicolor* (bicolor blenny) and *Salarius fasciatus* (jewelled rockskipper, or common algae blenny). Both species keep algae under control in the reef. Do not mix species of herbivorous blennies in the smaller aquarium as this can lead to fighting. Planktivores can be typified by *Ecsenius midas* (Midas blenny), an endearing, colorful species.

◀ *The bicolor blenny* (Ecsenius bicolor) *swims actively in the water column in pursuit of food and then reverses back into its retreat to survey its surroundings from a safe vantage point.*

▶ *The beautiful Red Sea mimic blenny* (Ecsenius gravieri) *mimics the blue-headed canary blenny* (Meiacanthus nigrolineatus), *which has venomous fangs. However, the mimic is harmless and hardy, peaceful, and full of character.*

FANG BLENNIES

The genus *Meiacanthus* contains a number of species known as fang blennies because of the very large canine teeth, with a venom gland at their base, found on the lower jaw. The Indo-Pacific *M. atrodorsalis* is mimicked by a yellow and blue form of *Ecsenius bicolor*.

* In the absence of the mimicked species, Ecsenius gravieri will remain almost exclusively on the rocks. It is not necessary to maintain the two species together.

BLENNIES

MIDAS BLENNY

The fascinating Midas blenny *(Ecsenius midas)* mimics the lyretail anthias *(Pseudanthias squamipinnis)*, swimming into open water with them and feeding on zooplankton. *E. midas* has separate color forms that are visible when it is resting, but these change when it is shoaling with the anthias. The Indonesian form of Midas blenny is the most variable in color, ranging from yellow-orange to green-brown.

▼ *The Midas blenny* (Ecsenius midas) *is often found in association with shoaling wreckfish* (Pseudanthias *spp.). It alternates between an open-water, highly active swimming style and prolonged periods of rest on the rocks.*

A DUAL PERSONALITY

If the algae blenny is confronted by a larger, more dominant fish in its territory, it may act shyly; but once that fish retreats, the algae blenny then bullies a fish smaller than itself. Its aggression is more apparent in a small aquarium.

▼ *The algae blenny* (Salarius fasciatus) *is popular with many aquarists because of its interesting behavior and because it consumes certain forms of filamentous algae and detritus. Given its large adult size (males 5.5 in [14 cm], females a little smaller), it will require a suitably sized aquarium (at least 66 gallons [250 liters]).*

Provide dried algae on a daily basis for the best results with this blenny. Many specimens will accept mysis and brine shrimp, among other meaty foods.

Gobies

Gobies tend to have large heads and mouths and cylindrical bodies. They often have a sucker on their undersides, formed from the fusion of the pelvic fins, that enables them to perch on vertical surfaces. Many species form commensal relationships with shrimps of the genus *Alpheus* and make a fascinating feature in any aquarium.

DIMINUTIVE AND POPULAR

At just 2 in (5 cm), female blue neon gobies are a little larger than males. Females are capable of changing sex, so if you intend to keep more than one individual, buy small ones or select two fish with a significant size difference. This species has been successfully bred in captivity.

The goby family is the largest group of marine fish, numbering more than 2,000 species.

▲ *The blue neon goby* (Elacatinus oceanops) *is a tiny cleaner fish that uses the fused pelvic fins to hold onto the fish it is cleaning. It then hops over the surface of the fish's body in search of dead skin or foreign bodies.*

The yellow prawn goby's coloration is highly variable, ranging from brilliant yellow to grey and even brown forms or combinations of each coloring.

▲ *The yellow prawn goby* (Cryptocentrus cinctus) *is the most widely available of all the gobies known to live in the burrows made by pistol shrimps (genus* Alpheus).

▶ *The dragon goby (Amblygobius phalaena) is a medium-large species (males and females 6 in [15 cm]) that makes an interesting alternative to gobies from the genus Valenciennea. It shares their sand-sifting behavior but is less prone to weight loss in the aquarium.*

This female dragon goby has a single spot on the tail fin. Males have a number of spots.

* *Many species of goby use their mouths to separate morsels of food from inedible sand, which they then expel through the gills. Species from the genus Valenciennea need several feeds a day of high-energy mysis shrimp or chopped shellfish to satisfy their nutritional needs.*

THE GOBY AND THE SHRIMP

The shrimp digs a burrow and the goby stands guard over the entrance. Should danger threaten, both retreat quickly into the tunnel. Industrious shrimp can create a network of interconnected chambers, so be sure to secure the rocks firmly.

Males and females grow to 2.5 in (6 cm). They have large mouths that gape when the fish are threatened.

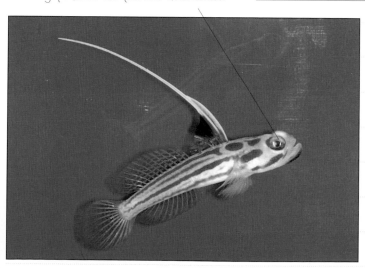

◀ *The stunning white-rayed shrimp goby (Stonogobiops yasha) is becoming easier to obtain but remains expensive. It forms a symbiotic relationship with the alpheid pistol shrimp Alpheus randalli. In the absence of a shrimp, the fish may not feed.*

COWFISH AND BOXFISH

Cowfish and Boxfish

Cowfish and boxfish are very similar groups, characterized by species in which the skeleton has become fused into a rigid structure containing all the internal organs. Cowfish tend to enhance this protection with long spines, and both cowfish and boxfish secrete noxious venom from their skin. Nevertheless, they should not be housed with aggressive species. Do not be tempted by tiny individuals, which cannot deal very well with high water flow and need plenty of specialized attention to thrive.

▶ *When stressed or threatened, the longhorn cowfish* (Lactoria cornuta) *can exude a toxin that is lethal to all the aquarium inhabitants, including itself. In the wild, it would swim away from the danger, but this is not possible in the confines of an aquarium. House this peaceful species with equally tolerant tank mates.*

The body becomes more elongate with age, reaching 18 in (46 cm), even in the aquarium.

An alert specimen feeds well and often follows people as they pass the tank.

▲ *The longhorn cowfish's common name refers to the paired, hornlike projections over each eye, one pointing forward and one to the rear. The pectoral fins are used for propulsion and the tail as a rudder.*

FEEDING THE COWFISH

The longhorn cowfish is a specialized feeder that blows jets of water from its mouth to expose food items in the sandy substrate. These may include small burrowing mollusks, worms, and crustaceans. Although it may attempt this behavior in the aquarium, it will also accept food from the water column. Offer dried algae, mysis, brine shrimp, enriched formula food, and vitamin supplements.

◀ *The yellow boxfish (Ostracion cubicus) is both beautiful and popular but not easy to maintain in the aquarium. Feed it at least three times per day on meaty foods or an enriched formula diet. Provide continual access to dried algae.*

Adult yellow boxfish will dominate other fish in the tank. Provide robust tank mates that will not bother the boxfish.

Young specimens resemble little yellow dice, but their colors may fade in time.

◀ *Boxfish are often available as inexpensive, small juveniles but can be bullied by aggressive fish of any size. The defensive toxin they emit can prove lethal. Juveniles need plenty of hiding places.*

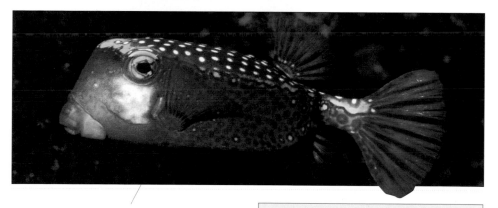

The male black boxfish is larger and more extravagantly patterned than the female.

▲ *The beautiful black boxfish (Ostracion meleagris) requires more care than most other commonly available species. This is another species that can emit a lethal toxin if stressed or threatened.*

BOXFISH PAIRS

Ostracion meleagris is one of the few boxfish species available in male-female pairs. Males (which grow up to 10 in [25 cm]) are more costly than female specimens (less than 6 in [15 cm]), but true pairs are expensive.

Miscellaneous species

Fish kept within the marine fish hobby include a number of species not closely related to one another or to those described elsewhere in this book. They include the dartfish, which swim actively in the water column; the substrate-dwelling dragonets; the predatory lionfish; and the fascinating pipefish.

◀ *The purple firefish* (Nemateleotris decora) *is a shy dartfish species that will hide in the rocks for long periods if it feels threatened. Make sure it gets enough to eat at feeding time.*

The stunning colors of this species have made it popular with aquarists.

AN EXPENSIVE RARITY

The third species in the genus *Nemateleotris* is *N. helfrichi*. In the wild, it is most commonly found in water at least 130 ft (40 m) deep and in the more remote tropical reefs of the world, which partly explains the high price it commands. However, given the right care, it will prove a hardy and long-lived aquarium specimen.

* *Dartfish are prone to leaping from uncovered aquariums and can escape through the tiniest hole. Take care when carrying out any work in the aquarium, as this can be stressful enough for the fish to begin leaping.*

▶ *Flame firefish* (Nemateleotris magnifica) *are best kept in male-female pairs. Housed with nonaggressive tank mates and fed on finely chopped shellfish, brine shrimp, and mysis, they should prove hardy in the aquarium.*

Despite its common name, this fish grows to about 6.7 in (17 cm) and may consume small tank mates.

▲ The fuzzy dwarf lionfish (Dendrochirus brachypterus) *is one of the most common species of venomous fish known as turkey fish or lionfish, and it is easy to keep in captivity. Small individuals, 1–1.5 in (3–4 cm), accept frozen brine shrimp and mysis. To encourage larger specimens to feed, you may need to wriggle small whole fish in the water.*

The clearfin becomes more active at feeding time or under blue actinic light.

* *Take care when moving rocks or cleaning the aquarium as this fish perches upside down under ledges during the day. Lionfish and scorpion fish are venomous and can inflict painful injuries.*

SIZE CONSIDERATIONS

The Fumanchu *(Dendrochirus biocellatus)* is another reasonably sized lionfish for the aquarium, reaching about 5 in (13 cm). Compare this with the imported turkey fish *(Pterois volitans)* which can reach a length of 20 in (50 cm), quickly outgrowing a small aquarium and viewing smaller tank mates as food.

▲ The clearfin lionfish (Pterois radiata) *grows to about 6.5 in (16 cm) in captivity. Try to choose a specimen that is feeding on dead food; it is possible to acclimatize newly imported specimens to frozen foods over time, but it is best to acquire one that already accepts these.*

MISCELLANEOUS SPECIES

Miscellaneous species (continued)

Although commonly referred to as scooters, or scooter blennies, these highly popular fish are not blennies (family Blennidae) but rather species of dragonet. The courtship of many dragonets can be observed in home marine aquariums, and they will often spawn.

◀ *The pink scooter dragonet, or blenny (Synchiropus ocellatus), will thrive where there is plenty of live rock harboring natural populations of the copepods and amphipods that it loves to eat. It will also pick frozen foods such as brine shrimp from sandy substrates.*

Scooter blennies are highly variable in color, ranging from almost brown to bright pink and red.

▶ *The male spotted mandarin dragonet (Synchiropus picturatus) is fiercely aggressive toward other males, but male-female pairs engage in fascinating courtship and spawning displays, which can take place regularly in most aquariums.*

◀ *In common with other* Synchiropus *species, the psychedelic mandarin dragonet (Synchiropus splendidus) relies on the presence of live rock to encourage the existence of small, self-sustaining populations of its natural food. Introducing similar species may mean they out-compete each other for the available food.*

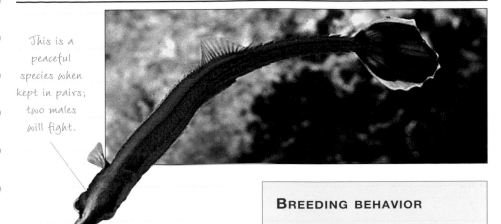

This is a peaceful species when kept in pairs; two males will fight.

▲ *The blue and orange cleaner pipefish* (Doryrhamphus excisus) *is fairly easy to keep in captivity. Offer it frozen brine shrimp and mysis, but make sure the food is small enough for the fish's tiny mouth. This pipefish acts as a cleaner fish, removing parasites from larger fish. Do not house it with predatory species.*

BREEDING BEHAVIOR

Male cleaner pipefish have bumps or notches on the snout, while the female's snout is smooth. Females deposit eggs in a brooding pouch located at the base of the tail on the underside of the male fish. The eggs are supplied with oxygen by the rich blood supply of the pouch lining. The larvae are difficult to rear.

SEA HORSES

Sea horses generally require high water quality and plenty of food. Since they are currently the subject of CITES restrictions, the vast majority of specimens on sale will be tank raised. These should be feeding on frozen food, which makes it much easier to keep them. Live foods can be difficult to obtain in sufficient quantities year-round. A species aquarium housing several individuals suits them best, with a lack of strong water flow and plenty of holdfasts in the form of artificial corals, algae, or gorgonians.

▶ *The yellow sea horse* (Hippocampus kuda) *grows to 10 in (25 cm). Mature males have a breeding pouch into which the female deposits her eggs. While raising this species is not difficult, it does require some dedication and can be time consuming.*

MISCELLANEOUS SPECIES

Invertebrates

A modern marine aquarium is capable of providing excellent accommodation for a wide variety of invertebrates, including corals. This section looks at a small sample of some of the most commonly available species. Be sure to obtain accurate information about the species that interest you before you buy them.

▲ *Blue tubular sponges are difficult to maintain unless your aquarium is capable of meeting their requirements exactly.*

▲ *The red and blue forms of the popular* Actinodiscus *sp. mushroom anemone are hardy and easy to keep.*

▲ *Mushrooms, such as this* Rhodactis *sp., are hardy and undemanding. They tolerate slow water currents and spread readily.*

▶ *Although not easy to maintain, the bubble anemone (*Enta cm)aea quadricolor*) is one of the hardier host anemones.*

◀ Giant button polyps (Palythoa grandis) are mostly available in shades of green and brown. This coral is undemanding but does best under strong lighting.

▶ Bush corals photosynthesize but will do best when fed. They can grow very large in the home aquarium.

▶ The ever-popular Lobophytum leather corals are easy to maintain but can secrete certain chemicals that inhibit the growth of their tank mates.

▼ Toadstool leather corals Sarcophyton sp. vary in the length and color of their polyps. Provide strong illumination.

▲ Branching soft corals, such as Cladiella sp., can grow very large very quickly. Give them plenty of room in the aquarium.

Invertebrates (continued)

▲ *Large polyp stony (LPS) corals are generally easier to maintain than small polyp stony (SPS) corals. This is a spiny brain coral,* Lobophyllia *sp.*

▼ *Hammer coral is a member of the genus* Euphyllia, *named for the unique shape of its polyps.*

STINGING CORALS

Coral reefs are tough places to eke out an existence, especially if you are rooted to the spot as many corals are. Many species have strong defenses in the form of specialized cells that are capable of inflicting painful stings. *Euphyllia* species can sting rival corals from a distance. Take care around such corals, and wash your hands if you come into contact with them.

◀ *The tentacles of the cornet coral (Euphyllia glabrescens) are capable of stinging their neighbors, so give this species plenty of room for expansion and growth.*

INVERTEBRATES

▶ *Tube, fan, or feather duster worms, such as this* Sabellastarte *species, are inexpensive and commonly available. Tube worms and corals differ in that corals derive much of their food from symbiotic algae. These are contained in their tissues and utilize the strong lighting available in the reef aquarium to synthesize sugars. Tube worms, however, must obtain their nourishment from fine particles in the water column. There are several commercially available kinds of invertebrate diet for these animals.*

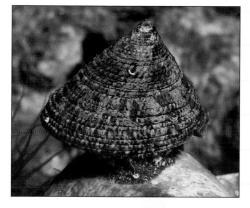

◀ *Herbivorous snails from the genus* Trochus *can grow large in the aquarium but are invaluable in the control and prevention of unwanted forms of algae. It is often useful to add a few species of herbivorous snail to the aquarium as each often shows preferences for different forms of alga.* Astraea *and* Turbo *snails are particularly good additions.*

▶ Tridacna maxima *clams not only filter fine particles of food from the water but also contain photosynthetic pigments in their mantles—the thin area of tissue that stretches over each side of the shell.*

Invertebrates (continued)

INVERTEBRATES

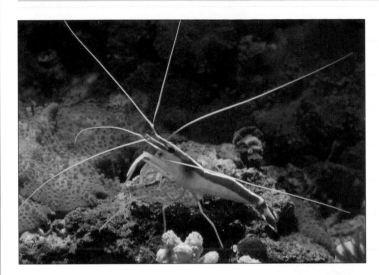

◀ *Skunk cleaner shrimps* (Lysmata amboinensis) *scavenge uneaten food intended for their vertebrate tank mates.*

▼ L. debelius *is less likely to stray into the open than* L. amboinensis *is, but it gains confidence with time.*

CHOOSE THE RIGHT SHRIMP

Beware of being wrongly sold candy, or dancing, shrimps *(Rhynchocinetes durbanensis)* as peppermint shrimps. These are not reef friendly and eat polyps. *R. durbanensis* has a red body with prominent white stripes, absent in *L. wurdemanni.*

◀ *Peppermint shrimp* (L. wurdemanni) *can serve a useful role by consuming the pest anemone species* Aiptasia.

◀ *The blue-knuckled hermit crab* (Calcinus elegans) *is a dwarf species that seldom proves problematic to keep in the aquarium.*

* Provide spare shells of varying sizes for all hermit crabs. Without them, fighting may ensue over suitable shells.

▲ *The scarlet hermit crab, or red-legged hermit, is very useful at preventing unwanted algae.*

▲ Neopetrolisthes *spp. anemone crabs prefer to live in stinging anemones. They trap food particles using netlike feeding appendages.*

▶ *Many shrimps from the genus* Alpheus *share their burrows with gobies.*

Invertebrates (continued)

▶ *Small serpent starfish, such as this* Ophiolepis *sp., make excellent scavengers. Large species or individuals can prey on fish and crustaceans.*

◀ *Species of serpent starfish range in color from dull brown or black to brilliant crimson.*

▼ *Handle long-spined sea urchins (*Diadema *spp.) with care. They grow quite large and are not suitable for the smaller aquarium.*

Many sea urchins need lots of calcium to grow, often at the expense of calcareous algae.

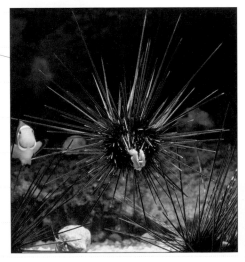

CLOSE RELATIVES

Urchins, starfish, and sea cucumbers are all echinoderms and therefore closely related, despite their very different appearances. Tunicates, or sea squirts, are distant relatives of all vertebrates, despite the resemblance of many species to simple sponges.

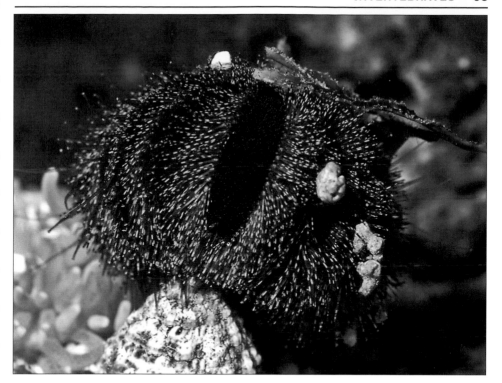

* Despite its common name, the spineless urchin has short dense spines.

▲ The spineless urchin (Mespilia globulus) is frequently found covered in debris of various sorts that serves as camouflage.

▼ Most tunicates, such as the giant Pacific tunicate, are filter feeders that require ample food to survive in captivity.

▲ The pink sea cucumber (Holothuria sp.) uses its short feeding tentacles to lift food particles from sandy substrates.

Picture credits

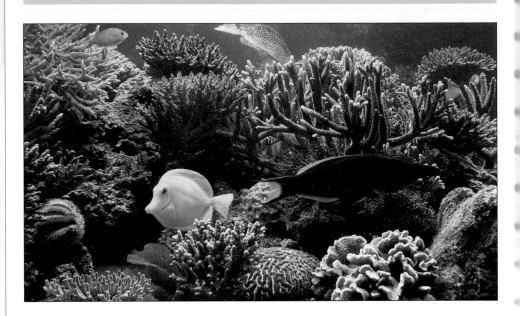

Additional picture credits

The publishers would like to thank the following photographers and companies for providing images, credited here by page number and position: T(Top), B(Bottom), C(Center), BL(Bottom left), etc.

Aqua Medic: 13(TR)

Aqua Press (M-P & C. Piednoir): 72(C), 83(B)

Bioquatic Photo—A.J. Nilsen, (www.biophoto.net): 5(BL), 32(BL), 34(BR), 37(BL), 45(BL), 56(TL,CR), 76(CR), 86(TL), 87(T,B), 90(TL), 91(BR), 93(CL,BR), 94(T,CL), 95(T,BR)

D-D Aquarium Solutions: 13(CL)

GHL Products: 11(TL)

Tim Hayes: 54(TR)

Lisa Page: All pictures pages 38–41, 69(T), 92(BL)

Photomax (Max Gibbs): 51(BR), 72(B), 88(TL)

Iggy Tavares: 79(B), 80(T), 81(T)

Kevin Webb: 63(BL)